which seek to reinterpret the old foundations to meet modern demands.

"Between militant Hinduism o[illegible] and aggressive secularism on the [illegible] many shades of thought and ac[illegible] should not be forgotten that w[illegible] resurgent Hinduism itself there are various trends differing from each other in ideological foundation, method of interpretation, and practical application.

"Radhakrishnan's significance, in this context, lies in the fact that he is not merely a philosopher, but also a responsible statesman actively participating in the life of his country. As President of the Republic of India, he brings to this exalted office wide scholarship, deep thought, mature experience, broad vision, and a profound concern for the life of the nation in the world of today.

"Although he is rooted in the national heritage of the country, he seeks to go beyond its narrow confines to the larger horizons of international understanding. In a considerable measure therefore, to understand Radhakrishnan's thought is to understand the new outlook that is slowly shaping itself in India and elsewhere . . .

"If this slight volume should help the student and the general reader to move beyond its limited confines to the larger works of Radhakrishnan himself and, therefore, to a more serious study of contemporary movements in India, the time and effort put into the writing of this book would be more than rewarded."

—S. J. Samartha

THE AUTHOR

Dr. S. J. Samartha was educated at the University of Madras, which granted him his degree in Economics and History. After completing his basic theological training at the United Theological College, Bangalore, he worked for several years as a lecturer in systematic theology and the history of religions.

Selected to go abroad for further studies, he did post-graduate work at Union Theological Seminary, New York, at the Hartford Seminary Foundation, Hartford, Conn., and at the University of Basel in Switzerland. His dissertation, *The Hindu View of History: Classical and Modern,* was published in India. He has contributed to learned journals in India and other countries.

Dr. Samartha is presently the Professor of Philosophy and History of Religions at the United Theological College, Bangalore, India, and also serves as the General Editor of the Christian Students' Library, a basic textbook series published for the Senate of Serampore University.

Of Dr. Samartha's ability to deal impartially with Radhakrishnan, an outstanding U.S. authority on the Indian President's philosophy comments: "Dr. Samartha has done an unusually objective kind of interpreting here—something which is all the more remarkable because he, obviously, is a Christian theologian (even though of Hindu background) . . . He has made a serious and sympathetic attempt to *understand* Radhakrishnan. This aspect shines through on almost every page of his work."

INTRODUCTION TO Radhakrishnan

THE MAN AND HIS THOUGHT

INTRODUCTION TO

THE MAN AND

NEW YORK

Radhakrishnan

HIS THOUGHT

By S. J. SAMARTHA

Professor of Philosophy

and History of Religions

United Theological College

Bangalore, South India

ASSOCIATION PRESS

INTRODUCTION TO RADHAKRISHNAN—
THE MAN AND HIS THOUGHT

Association Press, 291 Broadway, New York, N.Y. 10007

Seminary Paperback stock number: W439
Price, $2.25 paper
Publisher's hard-bound book stock number: 1541
Price, $4.50 cloth

Library of Congress catalog card number: 64–11596

Printed in the United States of America

This book is dedicated
To
The Memory of My Father

Acknowledgments

Grateful acknowledgment is made to the following publishers for permission to quote from books of which they own the copyright, more particularly to Allen & Unwin, Ltd., London, who have published most of Radhakrishnan's works.

Allen & Unwin, Ltd., London: *Kalki; Indian Philosophy,* Volume II; *The Hindu View of Life; An Idealist View of Life; Contemporary Indian Philosophy,* Muirhead and Roth, eds.; *Religion and Society; The Bhagavadgītā;* and *The Brahma Sūtra*—all by S. Radhakrishnan.

Oxford University Press, London: *Christian Faith and Other Faiths,* by Stephen Neill.

Clarendon Press, London: *Eastern Religions and Western Thought,* by S. Radhakrishnan.

Student Christian Movement Press, London: *A Faith for This One World?,* by Lesslie Newbigin.

Harper & Row, Publishers, Inc., New York: *The Recovery of Faith,* by S. Radhakrishnan.

The Westminster Press, Philadelphia: *Religion and the Christian Faith,* by Hendrik Kraemer.

The Library of Living Philosophers, Box 268, Wilmette, Illinois: *The Philosophy of Sarvepalli Radhakrishnan,* Paul A. Schilpp, ed.

Lutterworth Press, London: *The Concept of Maya,* by P. D. Devanandan.

If by inadvertence any permission which ought to have been obtained has been overlooked, apology is made to the holders of copyright, and thanks expressed to them for use of their material quoted in this book.

Preface

THIS BOOK IS AN INTRODUCTION to the essentials of Radhakrishnan's thought. Books written by Radhakrishnan are easily available, but the general reader or the student of philosophy will hardly find a single book which, within a brief compass, gives a survey of the fundamentals of Radhakrishnan's thought. *Introduction to Radhakrishnan* aims to meet this need. Although its major concern is with an exposition of Radhakrishnan's teachings, its purpose is not merely expository; for critical interpretation also forms a necessary part of this work. In the present dialogue between the East and the West at all cultural levels and in the encounter between world faiths today, it is necessary to have both a fair exposition and a responsible appraisal of differing points of view. Without this, mere friendliness will not lead to deeper understanding.

The importance of Radhakrishnan both as a representative of the renaissance of modern India and as one of the interpreters of its religio-philosophic foundations cannot be overestimated. It is true that in the complex cultural life of our country today other trends are also discernible which seek to reinterpret the old foundations to meet modern demands. Between militant Hinduism on the one hand, and aggressive secularism on the other, there are many shades of thought and action. Further, it should not be forgotten that within resurgent Hinduism itself there are various trends differing from each other in ideological foundation, method of interpretation, and practical application. Radhakrishnan's significance, in this context, lies in the fact that he is not merely a philosopher, but also a responsible statesman actively participating in the life of his country. As President of the Republic of India, he brings to this exalted office wide scholarship, deep thought, mature experience, broad vision, and a profound concern for the life of the nation in the world of today. Although he is rooted in the national heritage of the country, he seeks to go beyond its narrow confines to the larger horizons of international understanding. In a considerable measure therefore, to understand Radhakrishnan's thought is to understand the new outlook that is slowly shaping itself in India and elsewhere.

My indebtedness to friends and colleagues whose interest, encouragement, and advice have helped me in the preparation of this book cannot be adequately expressed. The substance of these chapters has been given several times in the form of lectures at the United Theological College, Bangalore, to students from India and abroad. The questions and observations of my students and the responsible comments of my colleagues have always been highly stimulating. The late Dr. P. D. Devanandan, formerly Director of the Christian Institute for the Study of Religion and Society, Bangalore, and Mr. M. M. Thomas, its present Director; my colleagues Dr. R. V. Spivey, Dr. K. Baago, and Dr. M. H. Harrison; also Dr. V. C. Samuel and Dr. E. L. Wenger of Serampore College, Serampore; and Mr. D. K. Sebastian of Bishop Cotton Boys' School, Bangalore—all these have gone through the manuscript of this book wholly or in part and have made many suggestions for improvement. Professor M. Yamunacharya, formerly of the University of Mysore, and Prof. C. T. K. Chari, Chairman of the Department of Philosophy, Madras Christian College, have kindly read the manuscript and have made helpful observations about certain points of interpretation. Thanks are also due to Mr. M. S. Balasubramaniam who typed the manuscript with scrupulous attention to details. Although I am expressing my thanks to all these friends, it must be said that I alone am responsible for the final form of this book and for any errors of interpretation or judgment that remain.

To Mr. N. G. Joseph, Literature Secretary of the National Council of YMCAs in India and to Mr. James Rietmulder, Director of the Association Press, New York, I owe a special word of thanks for the interest they have shown and the trouble they have taken to bring out an Indian and an American edition of this book.

If this slight volume should help the student and the general reader to move beyond its limited confines to the larger works of Radhakrishnan himself and, therefore, to a more serious study of contemporary movements in India, the time and effort put into the writing of this book would be more than rewarded.

—*S. J. Samartha*

United Theological College
Bangalore

Contents

1. *The Making of a Philosopher*

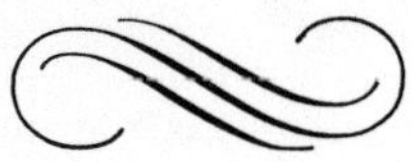

AMONG THE CONTEMPORARY THINKERS of India, Sarvepalli Radhakrishnan is well-known both in his home-land and in the West. As a philosopher, in recent years as a statesman and now as President of the Republic of India, he has made the most effective contribution to the West's understanding of India's thought and life. During a period of nearly fifty years, through his lectures, articles, and books, Radhakrishnan has presented to the world at large the best in ancient Hindu thought in the most attractive light possible, and in doing so he has also worked out a system of his own. There are many reasons for his importance in modern India. He is a philosopher-statesman who has effectively combined the task of a thinker with the responsibilities of a statesman. He has consistently defended Hinduism against all criticisms which tend to describe it as nonhistorical and negative. Among contemporary thinkers he has done a great deal to shape what may be described as a "world philosophy," by bringing Eastern and Western thought closer together. Further, Radhakrishnan represents the resurgent spirit of modern Hinduism asserting itself in the world of today, with a message which claims universal validity and world-wide application.

FORMATIVE FACTORS

Among the saints and thinkers of modern India, there are many about whom volumes have been written, giving details of their childhood, describing the activities of their youth, and emphasizing the accomplishments of their mature years. Very often, these accounts are merely descriptive and almost always uncritical in their evaluation. Radhakrishnan has consistently refused to write his autobiography and, even when requested by responsible editors, he has politely declined to give biographical details. However, it is not altogether impossible to have some idea of the general lines of what may be described as his intellectual autobiography. In a volume entitled *Religion in Transition*[1] Radhakrishnan has written such an autobiography significantly described as "My Search for Truth." Moreover, in his essay entitled "The Religion of the Spirit and the World's Need," he draws attention to some of the formative factors which have contributed to the shaping of his philosophic thought.[2]

Radhakrishnan was born in 1888 in Tirutani, a small town in South India. His parents were orthodox Telugu Brahmins who brought him up in the traditional pattern of Hindu life and practice. Tirutani was, and even today is,

---

1 Edited by Vergilius Ferm, 1937. A reprint of this essay was brought out by Shiva Lal Agarwala and Co., Ltd., Agra, 49 pp., in 1946.

2 See *The Philosophy of Sarvepalli Radhakrishnan,* The Library of Living Philosophers, P. A. Schilpp, Ed. (La Salle, Ill.: The Open Court Publishing Company, 1952). Essays by different authors on the various aspects of Radhakrishnan's thought. The first chapter, written by Radhakrishnan himself, has the subtitle—Fragments of a Confession, hereafter referred to as "Fragments"; and the last chapter is his reply to critics, hereafter referred to as "Reply." Copyright held by The Library of Living Philosophers.

a center of religious pilgrimage; and it is not difficult to see how his early outlook was in some measure influenced by the religious life around him. After finishing his early schooling, he spent the next twelve years of his life in Christian missionary institutions—Lutheran Mission High School, Tirupati (1896–1900); Voorhees' College, Vellore (1900–1904); and the Madras Christian College (1904–1908). His acquaintance with the Bible and, to some extent, with Church History and Christian Theology he owes to the years of study in these institutions in which, according to his own testimony, he grew up "in an atmosphere where the unseen was a living reality." However, he also points out that his uncritical faith in traditional Hinduism was shaken as a result of the criticism leveled against it by his teachers. It also upset him as a believing Hindu. He writes:

> My pride as a Hindu, roused by the enterprise and eloquence of Swami Vivekananda, was deeply hurt by the treatment accorded to Hinduism in missionary institutions. It was difficult for me to concede that Hindu ascetics and teachers who preserve for our world a living contact with the classical culture of India, which is at the root of most that we know and almost all that we practise, are not truly religious.[3]

His considered judgment on his teachers and the education he got is contained in a later statement in which he observes:

> My teachers in Christian missionary institutions . . . restored for me the primordial situation in which all philosophy is born. They were teachers of philosophy, commentators, interpreters, apologists for the Christian way of life and thought, but were not, in the strict sense of the term, seekers of truth.

[3] "My Search for Truth," 1946, p. 5.

By their criticism of Indian thought they disturbed my faith and shook the traditional props on which I leaned.[4]

Two points stand out in this statement. First, a clear recognition that traditional patterns of thought and life, merely because they have the sanction of ancient usage, need not necessarily be of relevance to meet the present needs. All through his life, therefore, Radhakrishnan has sought to go back to the original sources of ancient values and has actively devoted himself to prove that "the great insights, fundamental motives and patterns of thought of Hindu religion have meaning for us even today." Thus he points out that responsible criticism of Hinduism should not be ignored, but seriously considered, even though such criticism might come from alien quarters with motives other than mere academic interest. The second point is the description of his teachers as apologists and not "seekers of truth." It is not easy to understand this statement, particularly when one recalls the sincerity, the depth of devotion, and the profound scholarship in both Hindu and Christian classics, of some of the teachers who were connected with these institutions. Although it is true that they were committed to the Christian way of life, it is difficult to argue that they did not possess "the discipline of mind" and "a rigorously logical manner" which, according to Radhakrishnan, are "the essential means for the discovery of truth." There is obviously a difference in point of view and motives. One should also note the difference in one's understanding of "truth" in different contexts. To Radhakrishnan truth in this context seems to be more a state of being (*sat*), than one of cognition; and experiencing the truth, therefore, is more important than know-

[4] "Fragments," p. 9.

ing it. This explains the strong emphasis on *Svānubhava* in the thought of Radhakrishnan and others. More attention will be given to this question later.

From 1909 for seven years Radhakrishnan worked as a teacher of philosophy in the Madras Presidency College. These years gave him the opportunity not only to teach, but also to study the great classics of Eastern religions and Western thought. He studied the *Upanishads,* the *Bhagavadgītā* and the commentaries on the *Brahma Sūtra* by the great *acharyas* (teachers)—Sankara, Rāmānuja, Madhva, and others,[5] along with the classical writings of Buddhism and Jainism. Among the Western thinkers Plato, Plotinus, Kant, Bradley, and Bergson have influenced him greatly. Also, living at a time when India was seething with political and religious ferment, it is no wonder that he was much influenced by his contemporaries like Tagore and Gandhi, with whom he maintained a friendly relationship for more than thirty years.

Though Radhakrishnan was certainly stimulated by these thinkers and though he has incorporated some of their insights into the structure of his thought, one important source which, more than any other, has contributed to the making of this philosopher is his own authority, experience, and reflection. Drawing pointed attention to this factor he writes:

For my thinking had another source and proceeded from my own experience, which is not quite the same as what is acquired by mere study and reading. It is born of spiritual experience rather than deduced from logically ascertained premises. Philosophy is produced more by our encounter with

---

[5] His most recent work is a commentary on *The Brahma Sūtra* which bears the subtitle: The Philosophy of Spiritual Life (London: Allen & Unwin, Ltd., 1960).

reality than by the historical study of such encounters. In my writings I have tried to communicate my insight into the meaning of life . . . to foster the life of the spirit.[6]

This emphasis on mystical experience as the source and goal of life is repeatedly stressed in Radhakrishnan's writings. It also determines for him the purpose of philosophy as a discipline which is not just academic but which in its implications is also practical. "Philosophy is committed to a creative task. Although in one sense philosophy is a lonely pilgrimage of the spirit, in another sense it is a function of life."[7]

Radhakrishnan did not make up his mind very early to devote his life to the pursuit of philosophy and religion. As a young student at college, when he was wondering what particular subject to choose among five possible options, a cousin of his, who had just completed his studies, gave him his textbooks on philosophy. This, remarks Radhakrishnan, determined his life's vocation. Thus, what was apparently a mere accident determined his future interests; and gradually the study of philosophy became his lifework, sustaining him both intellectually and spiritually. Looking at the events which influenced his life and shaped his interests he observes:

I am persuaded that there is more in this life than meets the eye. Life is not a mere chain of physical causes and effects. Chance seems to form the surface of reality, but deep down other forces are at work. If the universe is a living one, if it is spiritually alive, nothing in it is merely accidental.[8]

After some years of work as professor of philosophy in

---

6 "Fragments," p. 10.
7 *Ibid.,* p. 6.
8 *Ibid.,* p. 6.

Mysore University, he was later appointed vice-chancellor of Banaras Hindu University. His appointment as Spalding Professor of Eastern Religions and Ethics at Oxford University was unprecedented in the sense that it was the first time that an Asiatic had been appointed to an Oxford Chair, and Radhakrishnan was deeply conscious of his responsibilities in that high office. In his Oxford lectures which he later published under the title *Eastern Religions and Western Thought* (see Selected Bibliography), Radhakrishnan pointed out that rather than being a subject of respectful but distant homage, the best in Hindu thought ought to be a matter of living concern to people in the West. During these years from 1936–1938 at Oxford, his own task which he responsibly accepted for himself was "to lift Eastern thought from its sheltered remoteness and indicate its enduring value as a living force in shaping the soul of the modern man."[9] There is no doubt that during these and subsequent years he has done a great deal to achieve this object. It is remarkable that along with such intellectual activity, he has combined practical responsibilities. As Ambassador to Russia, as Chairman of UNESCO and now as President of the Republic of India, Radhakrishnan is a living example showing that a life of contemplation need not necessarily be divorced from a life of action. As the President of the Republic of India, occupying the highest and most respected position in the country, Radhakrishnan has brought to his work a depth of thought, breadth of vision, and mature understanding of human problems, thus largely fulfilling Plato's ideal of a philosopher-king.

---

[9] *Eastern Religions and Western Thought* (Oxford, Eng.: The Clarendon Press, 1939), p. 20. This extract and others which follow are used by permission of The Clarendon Press. See C. E. M. Joad, *Counter Attack from the East* (London: Allen & Unwin, Ltd., 1933).

THE SIGNIFICANCE OF RADHAKRISHNAN

There are many reasons for the importance of Radhakrishnan in modern India. He is both a product of and a contributor to the Indian renaissance in general and to the Hindu resurgence in particular. His is a serious attempt to bring together the insights of the East and the West in a reasonable harmony. He is an apologist for and a defender of Hinduism against all forms of attack. He is a strong advocate of the message of Neo-Vedānta claiming universal validity and application.

Radhakrishnan has been aptly described as the "liaison officer" between the East and the West. "With his unique dual appointment at Banaras and Oxford, like a weaver's shuttle he has gone to and fro between East and West, carrying a thread of understanding, weaving it into the fabric of civilisation."[10] Probably no other Indian thinker has done so much to make Hindu thought intelligible and attractive to Western readers, and no other contemporary Indian philosopher has drawn so many elements from Western thought and made use of them in the structure of his system as Radhakrishnan. Although a few conservative Indian critics have felt that in his interpretation of Hinduism, he is "thoroughly un-Indian" and "has forgotten what it is to be a Hindu and has, instead, become an Orientalist,"[11] such criticisms do not do justice to the totality of his thought or the sincerity of his purpose. It is generally accepted that he is one of the greatest modern exponents of Hindu thought, possessing the true hospitality of the Hindu mind and defending successfully not only the essen-

10 *The Philosophy of Sarvepalli Radhakrishnan, op. cit.*, p. 86. See also C. E. M. Joad, *Counter Attack from the East, op. cit.*

11 A. M. K. Coomaraswamy, article in *The Review of Religion*, Vol. VI, No. 2, pp. 129 ff.

tials of Hinduism but the spirit which lies behind all religions.[12] Even those who consider him as representing only one type of Hindu thought grant that on the scale of world-wide cultural contacts, Radhakrishnan is the man "who in our days holds out to the world the light of an ancient, serene, and sometimes mysteriously profound way of thinking and living."[13] His work is important not merely because he gives an attractive description of a "mysteriously profound way of thinking," but also because of his conscious attempt to construct a system of thought in which there is place for the insights of other thinkers, both philosophers and scientists of the modern world. There are those who strongly maintain that the metaphysics of Radhakrishnan is a real fusion of the East and the West, particularly because he attempts to answer responsibly the problem which has haunted philosophers and theologians of all time, namely, the relation between the Absolute of philosophy and the God of religious experience. In his attempt to work out a solution to this problem, he is rightly described as "not merely the distinguished exponent of a lofty spiritual philosophy . . . but as the initiator of a new synthesis."[14] This observation, made nearly thirty years ago, holds good even today and is fully justified when one takes into account the total output of Radhakrishnan's works.

Further, Radhakrishnan also represents the spirit of resurgent modern Hinduism which is becoming increasingly articulate and more confident and which claims that

---

12 D. S. Sarma, *The Renaissance of Hinduism* (Banaras: Banaras Hindu University Press, 1944), p. 585; see also Radhakrishnan's book *The Recovery of Faith,* p. 204, listed in Selected Bibliography.

13 Swami Agehananda Bharati, in *The Philosophy of Sarvepalli Radhakrishnan, op. cit.,* p. 479.

14 *Times Literary Supplement,* London, May 3, 1934, quoted in "Fragments," footnote, p. 47.

its message, if properly interpreted and rightly understood, will be effective for the ills of all mankind. Whereas in his earlier books like *The Reign of Religion in Contemporary Philosophy* (1920), *Indian Philosophy* (Vol. I, 1923, and Vol. II, 1927), and *The Hindu View of Life* (1927), (these and his other books mentioned in this paragraph appear in the Selected Bibliography), he was primarily concerned with the defense and exposition of Hindu thought, in his later books he has made an attempt to bring it into responsible contact with Western patterns of thinking, particularly with the problems of human living—social, political, and international. One can see this emphasis in such books as *An Idealist View of Life* (Hibbert Lectures for 1929), *East and West in Religion* (1933 and 1949), *Eastern Religions and Western Thought* (1939), *Religion and Society* (Kamala Lectures, 1942 and 1948), his commentary on the *Bhagavadgītā* and his "Fragments" and "Reply," in *The Philosophy of Sarvepalli Radhakrishnan* (1952). Two other books also must be mentioned in this connection. One is *The Recovery of Faith* (1955), in which Radhakrishnan emphasizes that the fundamental need of the world at present is a spiritual reawakening, justifying the title—a recovery of faith. *The Brahma Sūtra* (1960) *which bears* the subtitle: "The Philosophy of Spiritual Life," is a work of his mature years, originating from experience, authority, and reflection. Radhakrishnan says that this book was born out of vital urges and under the pressures of concrete historical circumstances. It is an attempt to present "a reasoned faith" to meet the demands of the modern age. In his presentation of Hinduism he does not hesitate to use terms familiar to Western thinkers. This is one of the reasons why his works are intelligible to Western readers more easily than the writings of other Eastern thinkers. Although recognizing the limitations of the comparative method and not overlooking the different emphases in the East and in the West, Radhakrishnan points out that "the comparative method is relevant in the present context, when the stage is set, if not for the development of a world philosophy, at least for that of a world-outlook."[15]

Radhakrishnan has always emphasized that the spiritual message of Hinduism is adequate to meet not only the needs of India, but those of the whole of mankind. He writes:

> The great religious tradition of India which has had a continuous life from the seers of the Upanishads and the Buddha to Ramakrishna and Gandhi, may perhaps help to reintegrate this bruised, battered and broken world and give to it the faith for which it is in search.[16]

Again, he states that today, "Indian wisdom is essential not only for the revival of the Indian nation but also for the re-education of the human race."[17] Though admitting that it is absurd to speak of Indian monopolies of philosophic wisdom, he does maintain that the essential spirit of Hinduism is universally valid and its message worthy of world-wide application, because there is "one perennial and universal philosophy" to be found in all lands and cultures.

THE PURPOSE OF THE PHILOSOPHER

Though it is necessary to consider the factors which have contributed to the making of this philosopher-statesman, it is equally essential to take into account the purpose which

15 "Fragments," p. 13.
16 *Hibbert Journal,* Vol. XLIV, 1946, No. 4, p. 304.
17 "Fragments," p. 11.

he has set for himself. This purpose is born of his analysis of the human situation today and his firm faith that religion alone can provide the adequate remedy to cure the sickness of the age. India, in accepting the way of political democracy, is no longer a silent spectator of history, but an active participant in it. This means that in the midst of her frantic efforts to attain national unity, political stability, and economic prosperity, she cannot ignore questions relating to the nature and destiny of man, the structure of responsible society, the meaning of history, and the ultimate fate of mankind in the scheme of things. Resources have to be found to undergird her national philosophy. Among alternatives, secular humanism and religious philosophy are strong contenders for the loyalties of the individual and of the nation. Perhaps Radhakrishnan's greatest contribution and certainly the most far-reaching, is his attempt to work out the lines of a philosophy of spiritual life that should undergird the national quest for prosperity, stability, and peace.

There is a threefold emphasis in Radhakrishnan's writings which aims at fulfilling this purpose. First, one should note his analysis of the human situation and his firm conviction that religion alone can heal the sickness of the modern age. Second, is his definition of what this "religion" means. He is careful to point out that by religion he does not mean any particular faith, but the religion behind the religions, the *sanātana dharma.* And third, there is his claim that Neo-Hinduism, if it is rightly interpreted and properly understood, can provide the basis for this eternal religion which, though holding on to the tested and proved values of the past, can also make room for the values of other religions in a spirit of friendliness, tolerance, and harmony.

According to Radhakrishnan's analysis, mankind is still in the making, in search of spiritual perfection and "the new birth for which humanity awaits is a spiritualised humanity."[18] The present sickness of the world is the birth pang of a new religion. In the present travail of civilization "the world's unborn soul is struggling to be born" and "the supreme task of our generation is to give a soul to the world consciousness."[19] Various factors have contributed to the breakdown of modern civilization. The scientific outlook, technological developments, and secular humanism have in differing degrees shaken the faith of man in the values of traditional religions. Most of these antireligious factors are merely symptoms of a revolt against the wrong kind of religious emphasis. "Humanism is a legitimate protest against those forms of religion which separate the secular and the sacred, divide time and eternity and break up the unity of soul and flesh."[20] Because unity has been so profoundly disturbed, there is disintegration both in the soul of man and in the heart of civilization. The sense of values is blurred, the conception of ends and means is confused, and the future is uncertain. There is incoherence in thought and indecision in action. This, however, need not fill man with despair. Inadequate alternatives have to be rejected. Neither a contented fatalism nor a complacent satisfaction is worthy of acceptance. In place of *bhaya* (fear) mankind is in great need of *abhaya* (freedom from fear). Anxiety should give place to faith, and inward discord to spiritual harmony; and religion alone can fulfill this task. "We need a rational

---

18 "Reply," p. 805.

19 *Eastern Religions and Western Thought, op. cit.,* Preface, p. 8.

20 *The Recovery of Faith* (New York: Harper & Row, Publishers, Inc., 1955), p. 49.

faith to sustain a new order of life."[21] Elaborating this point, Radhakrishnan writes:

We need a philosophy, a direction and a hope, if the present state of indecision is not to lead us to despair. Belief may be difficult, but the need for believing is inescapable. We are in search of a spiritual religion, that is universally valid, vital, clear-cut, one that has an understanding of the fresh sense of truth and the awakened social passion which are the prominent characteristics of the religious situation today.[22]

However, this "spiritual religion" which alone can give healing power for mankind, is not confined to any one particular faith. Ignorance of the values of other religions should not lead the adherents of one specific religion to make monopolistic claims. This is repeatedly emphasized by Radhakrishnan and is often directed against those religions which, according to him, make exclusive claims for their particular message. He points out that today, with the whole world as one's cultural base, it would be "an academic error, a failure in perspective" to limit oneself only to the voices of Isaiah and Paul, Socrates and Cicero, for there are also others like the prophets of Egypt, the sages of China, and the seers of India, who, as guide posts, disclose to mankind the course of its trail.[23] All these sources must therefore be taken into account in shaping the eternal religion. "It is not to be identified with any particular religion, for it is the religion which transcends race and creed and yet informs all races and creeds."[24] Therefore, in the face of growing secularism, the different religions of mankind should participate in a common pil-

21 *Eastern Religions and Western Thought, op. cit.*, p. 19.
22 "Fragments," p. 25.
23 *Eastern Religions and Western Thought, op. cit.*, p. 20.
24 *The Recovery of Faith, op. cit.*, p. 204.

grimage on the road to "the larger religion of the spirit." This religion, says Radhakrishnan, "is not irrational or unscientific, is not escapist or anti-social. Its acceptance will solve many of our desperate problems and will bring peace to men of goodwill."[25]

In spite of this strong emphasis on the religion behind all religions, there is also a strong advocacy in Radhakrishnan of the claims of Hinduism, particularly of Vedānta. His argument seems to be that although in other countries and civilizations religion has been a part of man's quest of being, in India alone it has always been given a central place in life and thought. He says:

> Religion, however, has been the master passion of the Hindu mind, a lamp unto its feet and a light unto its path, the presupposition and basis of its civilisation, the driving force of its culture, and the expression—in spite of its tragic failures, inconsistencies, divisions and degradations—of its life in God.[26]

Whereas there are others who strongly question the general opinion contained in this statement regarding the primacy of religion in the evolution of India's life and culture, Radhakrishnan has consistently maintained this position all through the years. In his latest book, *The Brahma Sūtra,* he once again reiterates this theme when he describes his exposition of the religion based on this great Hindu classic as "a reasoned faith," "the philosophy of spiritual life," which is fully adequate to meet the demands of the modern age. There is thus an acknowledged purpose in Radhakrishnan's work, namely, to provide a faith in fundamentals at a time when the foundations of

---

25 "Fragments," p. 82.

26 *Eastern Religions and Western Thought, op. cit.,* pp. 20 ff., for a discussion of the claims of Hinduism in this respect.

human life are being shaken by revolutionary forces. At this significant period in the history of India the prevailing mood "is to search for the meaning of faith in the transforming power of the spirit over the downward drag of things, to find the significance of religion in a world where temporal, material values have lost their relationship to eternal, spiritual good."[27] Radhakrishnan's interpretation of Hinduism is one of the ablest efforts in contemporary India to indicate the meaning of faith and the significance of religion at the present time.

---

[27] P. D. Devanandan, *Living Hinduism: a Descriptive Survey* (Bangalore: Christian Institute for the Study of Religion and Society, 1958), pp. 2–3.

2. *Hinduism According to Radhakrishnan*

MODERN RELIGIOUS MOVEMENTS IN INDIA from the time of Raja Ram Mohan Roy (1772–1833) up to the present day, are, to a large extent, the result of an insistent demand that traditional religions should come to terms with contemporary needs. Among other things, the usefulness of the material values of life, the demand for social justice, the urgency of a political philosophy and the need for world solidarity, are factors which have been increasingly influencing the restatement of traditional religious beliefs. In his interpretation of Hinduism, Radhakrishnan has consistently kept these factors in mind. Whether it is in his strong defense of Hinduism against criticism or in his attempts to incorporate the insights of modern science and social thought into his system of thought or, in recent years, in his exegetical exposition of ancient Hindu classics like the *Upanishads,* the *Bhagavadgītā* and the *Brahma Sūtra,* Radhakrishnan has tried to interpret Hinduism in such a way as to make its enduring values consistently relevant to the needs not only of India, but of the world at large.

WHAT IS HINDUISM?

What is Hinduism, is a question more easily asked than answered. In a sense this is true of all attempts to define religion itself. It is easier to describe some of the characteristics of particular religions than to give a comprehensive definition of religion acceptable by all concerned. As far as Hinduism is concerned it is much more difficult. Among other reasons, this is partly because in India religion and culture are very closely interrelated and, partly, because in Hinduism the line of demarcation between philosophy and religion is exceedingly difficult to draw. Moreover, one should also keep in mind that Hinduism has no universally accepted canon of authoritative writings except, of course, the sectarian groups. This makes it more difficult to define Hinduism in its comprehensiveness. Archer has observed that "Hinduism is reckless of creed, tolerant of religious rivalries, and patient with heresies." Where tolerance, however, is claimed to be a great virtue, it is obvious that it will be difficult to find out what exactly constitutes orthodoxy and heresy in Hinduism. In a recent book,[1] Swami Nikhilananda remarks that "the universal nature of Hinduism frustrates any endeavour to confine it in exact statement." He goes on to say, however, that the cardinal tenets of Hinduism may be summarized as follows: the nonduality of the Godhead, the divinity of the soul, the unity of existence, and the harmony of religions.

Though these points are certainly important in Neo-Vedānta, of which the Swami is one of the ablest exponents in the West, the points which have been left out

[1] Swami Nikhilananda, *Hinduism: Its Meaning for the Liberation of the Spirit* (London: Allen & Unwin, Ltd., 1959), p. 25.

are by no means unimportant. When trying to understand modern interpretations, the historical evolution of Hinduism and the different periods in its cultural history should not be overlooked. This is necessary lest one should miss proper perspective; for modern interpretations are not to be considered in isolation, but as part of the whole story of Hinduism through the ages. The resurgence of Hinduism in modern India is one of the most creative movements in its history, although it should not be forgotten that the total pattern of Hinduism is larger than particular interpretations of it at any time. C. P. Ramaswamy Aiyar is right when he compares Hinduism to "a great golden umbrella, which shelters many forms of thought, many practices and many approaches to the divine . . . it has sheltered all forms of thought and speculation and is an umbrella which is still standing."[2] D. S. Sarma is more descriptive, both of its nature and its attitude, when he writes:

> Hinduism is more a league of religions than a single religion with a definite creed. In its hospitable mansion there is room for all types of souls from the highest to the lowest, and, as one grows in virtue, love and insight, one can pass from apartment to apartment and never feel that the atmosphere is stuffy or hot.[3]

And Radhakrishnan himself points out that Hinduism "is not a definite dogmatic creed, but a vast, complex, but subtly unified mass of spiritual thought and realisation."[4] All this is to emphasize the fact that at the present moment, what is important is not so much a *definition* of Hinduism

---

[2] *Indian Inheritance*, Bhavan Series, Volume I, K. M. Munshi and N. C. Aiyer, eds. (Bombay: Bhavan's Book University, 1955), p. 222.

[3] D. S. Sarma, *What Is Hinduism?* (Madras: Ganesh and Co., 1939), p. 10.

[4] *The Hindu View of Life* (London: Allen & Unwin, Ltd., 1927), p. 21.

as an *interpretation* of its essential message to the modern world. It is in this context that the work of a person like Radhakrishnan is highly significant, because he attempts to present the message of Hinduism in such a way that although its continuity with the past is maintained, its content is very much reinterpreted to meet modern demands.

Radhakrishnan's restatement of Hinduism is very closely related to his defense of it against charges from different quarters. In his earlier books particularly he took strong exception to criticisms made by certain Western scholars of both the content of Hinduism and the attitude toward life which it is said to inspire. Defense of Hinduism necessarily involves a justification of some of its classic exponents like Sankara and some of its major concepts like *Brahman, māyā,* and *karma.* The specific form of these interpretations will be considered later. At this point we are concerned with Radhakrishnan's defense of Hinduism in general and of Vedānta in particular.

Radhakrishnan has always been extremely sensitive to some of the criticisms made by Western scholars. In his earlier books he has vehemently defended Hinduism against the charges of world-negation and of a lack of ethical responsibility. The main points of his defense and, along with it, a restatement of Hinduism are expounded among other works, in his two volumes of *Indian Philosophy,* in *The Hindu View of Life,* and in *Eastern Religions and Western Thought.* It is essential to call attention to these points, because in his later works also he comes back to the same theme and, though his tone is less aggressive, his arguments more informed, and his exposition more positive in content, the basic lines of his restatement are already drawn in these earlier works. He has strongly criticized certain Western scholars[5] for basing their criticisms on too general a classification of the world's great religions, contrasting Eastern and Western religions. Sometimes this contrast is stated as between *prophetic* religion and *mystic* religion. It is claimed that Christian thought is dynamic, active, and creative, characterized by a will to live and an outlook which is described as "world and life affirming." Hindu thought, on the other hand, is said to be quietistic and contemplative, with a tendency to deny the reality of the world and to escape from history, neglecting man's ethical responsibilities. It is claimed that the attitude it inspires is one of "world and life negation." When one takes into account the contemporary resurgence of Hinduism and the active participation of India in the history of the world, it is sometimes surprising that these criticisms are so often made against it in different forms even today. Therefore it would be helpful to consider Radhakrishnan's refutation of some of these points.

He emphatically rejects the criticism that Hinduism results in an attitude of life-negation in contrast to the attitude of life-affirmation. He points out that such "immense simplifications" do not do full justice to the complex pattern of life and history. Such clear-cut schemes and broad generalizations are often misleading, neither do they always mutually exclude each other. There are elements in Eastern thought which are world affirming and there are elements in Western thought which are world negating in character. The fact that at a particular stage in the life and history of a people, a particular attitude has been dominant, does not necessarily mean that it is the entire

5 Albert Schweitzer, *Indian Thought and Its Development* (Boston: Beacon Press, 1957) and Friedrich Heiler, *Prayer* (New York: Oxford University Press, 1958). See *Eastern Religions and Western Thought, op. cit.,* Chapter III, "Mysticism and Ethics in Hindu Thought," pp. 58 ff.

life philosophy of the people for all time. He admits that such a thing has happened in the evolution of Hinduism in India and recognizes a causal connection between "anaemic Hindu religion" and India's "political failure" in certain periods of her history.[6] But, he claims, this need not be so for all time and surely it is not so at the present moment of India's history. Radhakrishnan takes great pains to show that a positive attitude toward life and history can be developed on the basis of essential elements in Hindu thought and that it can be made responsibly relevant to the intellectual and social environment of today.

Moreover, to strengthen this basic point he draws attention to certain features in Hindu thought which, according to him, have always emphasized responsible action in a real world. The *varṇa dharma* (caste duties) and *āshrama dharma* (duties attached to the four stages of life) are surely not world and life negating. Moreover, the doctrine of *karma samsāra* is meaningless without some value being attached to man's individual responsibility for his actions in this world. Furthermore, the great Epics of Hinduism—the *Mahābhārata* and the *Rāmāyaṇa*—stress the duty and dignity of man, and the joy and responsibility of life in all its varied aspects. In his commentary on the *Bhagavadgītā,* Radhakrishnan elaborates this point and shows why this book has so much value and relevance for India today. The *Gītā* opens with a problem. It was a question of participating or not participating in the tremendous drama of history that was opening before Arjuna. He refuses to fight and raises all sorts of difficulties against the call of active participation and puts up a plea for inactivity and

[6] *Contemporary Indian Philosophy,* J. A. Muirhead and S. Rath, eds. (London: Allen & Unwin, Ltd., 1936).

retreat. The purpose of the *Gītā* is to convince Arjuna, who represents man in history, of the necessity for action. The *Bhagavān* of the *Gītā* patiently teaches Arjuna that action is necessary, provided one offers his work as worship to God. The message of the *Gītā* therefore is a message of action, not inaction, calling for participation in history, not beckoning man to a pilgrimage of retreat. Radhakrishnan maintains that although this emphasis might have been obscured in certain periods in the history of India, it will be sheer ignorance to say that such an attitude never existed in Hinduism. Thus the scriptural basis for responsible action is always there and one has only to look for it. The practical bearing of philosophy on life has commanded his interest from the beginning. Philosophy in India is not merely theoretical speculation, individual meditation, or the flight of the alone to the Alone. To Radhakrishnan philosophy must be concerned with the problems of human existence. "We are not contemplating the world from outside, but are in it."[7]

The question of the relation between contemplation and action, between the realm of the spirit and the realm of history, Radhakrishnan points out, is not a problem peculiar to Hinduism alone. It is a persistent problem one meets in the history of other religions also. He maintains that it is wrong to think that all contemplative seers are lacking in the practical sense of social responsibility. Sankara, in spite of the fact that he was a great philosopher, was also an effective organizer. The religious establishments—*maṭhs*—he founded in the four corners of India during the course of his travels stand even today as monuments to his practical ability and farsightedness. If one

[7] *Ibid.*, p. 258

considers the achievements in the field of action by the sages of India from the Buddha to Mahatma Gandhi and by the great mystics in the West like St. Paul, St. Theresa, and St. Francis, one will be struck by their capacity for responsible action in society. "They sink their roots in God and raise their branches in the world. If the divine is ultimate reality, contemplation is not an escapism."[8] However, Radhakrishnan is not arguing that the way of action is superior to the way of contemplation. What is necessary is a balance, a harmony, an integration of both, although at the present moment when technology seems to overshadow the humanities, he strongly emphasizes the need for contemplative leaders. He writes:

> The contemplative seers exercise great influence on society without deliberate calculation. Their gentle stillness is a rebuke to the noisy futility of our age, their restraint and renunciation a devastating criticism of its ambition and acquisitiveness. To assuage the bitterness and contradictions of our age we require men of detachment and dignity, of purposeful living and abundant humanity.[9]

THE RELEVANCE OF "ADVAITA"

Although Radhakrishnan has set for himself the lifelong task of defending Hinduism and giving a valid exposition of its essentials, yet, by both temperament and conviction he may be regarded as an Advaitin, a follower of the Sankarite school of Vedānta. While he was still a student at the Madras Christian College he wrote a thesis on the *Ethics of the Vedānta* which was highly commended by his teacher, Dr. A. G. Hogg. The apologetic motive was

---

8 "Reply," p. 803.
9 *Ibid.*, p. 804.

obvious in this work; and later, in his *Indian Philosophy,* he strongly defended the Vedānta of Sankara against the criticisms made by Hogg and others.[10] Radhakrishnan's significant contribution has been to give a philosophic justification to *Advaita Vedānta,* defending it against criticisms and bringing its message to meet the needs of the modern world. The points of defense he makes ought to be stated here mainly because in his later works he defines, elaborates, and justifies them, giving Vedānta a more positive content. The following is a brief summary of the criticisms and Radhakrishnan's response.

- If *Brahman* alone is all and the world is simply *māyā,* then moral distinctions are rendered meaningless and ethical actions seem to be unnecessary.—Radhakrishnan says that the sting of this criticism is based on the interpretation of *"māyā."* It is his contention that to Sankara the world is not just an "illusion," so that moral action in the world need not be considered meaningless or unnecessary.
- The *advaita* insistence on the metaphysical identity between the *Brahman* and the *Ātman* denies freedom and responsibility to the individual—and so cuts the root of all moral endeavor.—Radhakrishnan's answer is that this criticism is based on a confusion between reality and existence. The identity claimed by Vedānta is the identity of the real self, not the active self, with the *Brahman.* Therefore, the metaphysical truth of the oneness of the *Brahman* does in no wise prejudice the need for ethical distinctions on the *vyāvahārika* or empirical level.
- It is sometimes argued that Sankara's insistence that *avidyā,* ignorance, is the cause of all bondage, and that

10 See *Indian Philosophy* (London: Allen & Unwin, Ltd.), Vol. II, 1927, pp. 621 ff.

spiritual freedom consists in *jnāna,* enlightenment, is too intellectualistic to be ethically meaningful. According to him, salvation seems to be the result of metaphysical insight, not of moral perfection.—Radhakrishnan maintains that although to Sankara *avidyā* is primarily a logical concept, it actually signifies a whole attitude toward life, mistaking the relative to be the absolute, a mistaken notion which is the cause of bondage. False knowledge is self-conceit, the root of all selfish desire and activity. The state of freedom is the removal of this error, the suppression of all selfish desires and the restoration of true freedom. Moral life is necessary until *avidyā* is removed. Sankara does not emphasize mere learning, *pānditya;* he also points out the need for *chitta shuddhi,* purification of the heart, *bālya,* childlikeness, and *mauna,* silence that is born of the fullness of knowledge and joy. Therefore, far from denying the need for moral life, Sankara says that it is an essential discipline until *avidyā* is removed.

• This would, however, mean that to Sankara moral life is only relative and that ultimately it has no significance at all.—In answering this objection Radhakrishnan argues that moral distinctions are valid on the *vyāvahārika* level as long as the individuality of the finite self is maintained, but that on the *pāramārthika* level, moral distinctions have no relevance. However moral one might be, infinite perfection is beyond moral endeavor. *Moksha* can come only as the result of *jnāna. Avidyā,* which is the root cause of finiteness and separateness, must be overcome. The highest morality consists in developing the right spirit, and moral life is the necessary result of spiritual insight. The secret of moral genius lies "in the spiritualising of our consciousness."

• A further criticism of Vedānta is that it is far too

ascetic in its outlook and discipline.—Radhakrishnan admits that Sankara does emphasize the transitoriness of life and the need to keep the body under strict control, but he goes on to add that it is a misunderstanding of Sankara to say that his asceticism is a denial of the body as such. According to Radhakrishnan, Sankara "insists on a life of self-sacrifice and asks us to free ourselves from attachment to the body. The enemy of the soul is not the body as such, but our bondage to the body and the sense of mineness."[11]

• Another oft-repeated criticism of Sankara is that in the *advaita* view of life, there is no room for social responsibility or civic duty. The tendency for the individual is to escape from the world, not to participate in history with a sense of social duty.—Radhakrishnan's reply is that the very life and work of Sankara is a standing refutation of this criticism. "The emphasis in Sankara is not on retirement from the world, but on the renunciation of the self." What he asks us to suppress is selfishness; and, if that requires solitude and retirement, they are means to an end. The attitude Sankara advocates is one of being in the world, and yet not of it; for he who has shaken off selfishness is at liberty to work for the salvation of the world at large. The *jīvanmuktās,* far from going away from the strain and stress of the world, on the contrary continue in it in order to enable others to attain *moksha.*

• One more objection to the *advaita* of Sankara is that its conception of *moksha* is too negative. It is a state where all life is stilled, where individuality is no more and where personality ceases to exist.—In answer to this, Radhakrishnan points out that what happens at the end will always be a mystery, because it involves the relation between the *Brahman* and the world, the finite and the Infinite, the

---

11 *Ibid.,* p. 632.

temporal and the eternal. Though the world depends on the *Brahman* and finally all life goes back to its ultimate Source, how it happens one cannot say. Moral life and spiritual *moksha* surely cannot be divorced from each other; yet, how they are ultimately related cannot be described. Nor can it be said that the world is negated when the *Brahman* is reached. Sankara constantly says that this world has its roots in the *Brahman* and that the "pathway to the real lies through the phenomenal." Sankara's conception of *moksha* appears to be negative because positive terms do not, and cannot be used to, describe it.

Some of the points of criticism are obviously strong and cannot be so easily dismissed. It will be seen later that further argumentation and more careful justification are necessary to maintain the edifice of defense which Radhakrishnan puts up. Nevertheless, the general lines of his Neo-Vedānta are laid down here. In these arguments his strategy is already determined, and the battle lines drawn. The rest is mostly a work of bringing up reinforcements, extending the lines of action and consolidating the gains.

MAJOR CHARACTERISTICS OF HINDUISM

Radhakrishnan's positive exposition of some of the major doctrines of Hinduism will be considered in more detail at a later stage. Though closely following the pattern of Vedānta as expounded by Sankara, Radhakrishnan has so interpreted its major doctrines as to give its contents a new significance at the present moment. Some of the major characteristics of Hinduism as interpreted by Radhakrishnan should be considered as a prelude to a more detailed consideration of his fundamental teachings.

Radhakrishnan emphasizes the *comprehensiveness* of Hinduism. Hinduism, in the course of its long history, has been able to incorporate into its structure many varieties of beliefs and religious practices. Aryan and non-Aryan elements have been so blended as to give it an all-embracing unity. Therefore, one might rightly say that Hinduism "is a large comprehensive unity of a living organism with a fixed orientation."[12] Its intellectual resilience and innate spiritual strength help it to be "a vast, complex and subtly unified" system in which there is place for all types of beliefs and practices, from the highest to the lowest.

Further, Hinduism is *universal* in character, particularly because it stresses spiritual experience and inward realization which, by its very nature, cannot be confined to particular religions or countries. Spirit is "free being," and spiritual life is not bound by form. This characteristic makes it possible for Hinduism to grow, gathering unto itself the experience of saints from all over the world. Hinduism "is a movement, not a position; a process, not a result; a growing tradition, not a fixed revelation."[13]

Moreover, Hinduism is *nonhistorical* in character, because it does not depend upon any particular human founder or upon a set of historical facts. This, according to Radhakrishnan, far from being a limitation, is on the contrary a virtue, because it recognizes freedom in the matter of religious truth. The truth of Hinduism does not depend on the historicity of a particular founder and the shifting sands of historical criticism, but on "eternal truths." In his commentary on the *Gītā* he discounts the historicity of Krishna and makes him a type or a symbol of the higher self in man. He writes:

---

[12] *The Hindu View of Life, op. cit.*, p. 7.
[13] *Ibid.*, p. 129.

It is of little moment so far as the teaching is concerned, whether the author is a figure of history or the very god descended into man, for the realities of the spirit are the same now as they were thousands of years ago and the differences of race and nationality do not affect them. The essential thing is truth or significance and the historical fact is nothing more than the image of it.[14]

Tolerance is another characteristic virtue of Hinduism; and, because of this, claims Radhakrishnan, Hinduism alone can provide the true basis for a doctrine of the spiritual harmony of all religions. This point is strongly upheld in his different books and more recently elaborated by contemporary thinkers to maintain the equality of different religions. In the City of God citizenship should be open to all. "Tolerance is the homage which the finite mind pays to the inexhaustibility of the Infinite."[15] He quotes the *Rig Veda* in which it is said, "Truth is One, the sages call it many,"[16] and the *Bhagavata* which declares that "the One Supreme is conceived in different ways through different scriptural traditions."[17] The attitude of tolerance in Hinduism is not the result of ignorance or of skepticism, but of conviction, sympathy, and respect. "For a true Hindu there are few places dedicated to God in which he may not silently worship, few prayers in which he may not reverently join."[18]

Another characteristic of Hinduism, perhaps the more important one, is its stress on *anubhava—intuition.* Hinduism is "more a transforming experience than a notion of God."[19] In Hinduism, says Radhakrishnan, "intellect is

---

[14] *The Bhagavadgītā:* Introductory Essay (London: Allen & Unwin, Ltd., 1949), p. 37.

[15] *Eastern Religions and Western Thought, op. cit.,* p. 317.

[16] *Rig Veda,* i. 164, 46.

[17] *Bhagavata,* iii. 32, 33.

[18] *Eastern Religions and Western Thought, op. cit.,* p. 313.

[19] *Ibid.,* p. 21.

subordinated to intuition, dogma to experience, outer expression to inner realisation."[20] The foundation truths of the Hindu religion are the conclusions not of logical reasoning nor of an interpretation of historical facts, but products of *dristi,* born out of an encounter with reality.[21]

This question of intuition is one of the most elusive concepts in the structure of Radhakrishnan's thought covering a wide range. It is used in different senses in different contexts; and it is unfortunate, Radhakrishnan himself admits, that the single term "intuition" should be used to represent scientific genius, poetic insight, ethical conscience as well as religious faith. Even in Radhakrishnan's writings it is extremely difficult to limit it to the broad religious connotation alone. Browning's article "Reason and Intuition in Radhakrishnan's Philosophy," is a penetrative analysis of this question mainly from the philosophical point of view.[22]

In Radhakrishnan the word "intuition" is sometimes used to describe the *process* of knowing, particularly in his expositions of Indian philosophy and the *pramāṇas*. Sometimes it refers to the *product* of knowledge, the sum total of one's conception of God derived through a process of intuition. At other times, it denotes a particular *faculty* as, for example, when he speaks of *anubhava*—intuition; *tarka*—intellect; and *Śruti*—Scripture; a faculty which enables one to receive knowledge which it would not be possible to get otherwise. "The deepest convictions by which we live and think, the root principles of all thought and life are not derived from perceptual experience or logical

20 *The Hindu View of Life, op. cit.,* p. 15.

21 *An Idealist View of Life* (London: Allen & Unwin, Ltd., 1947), pp. 89, 127 ff., 138 ff.

22 See *The Philosophy of Sarvepalli Radhakrishnan, op. cit.,* pp. 448 ff. See also *The Brahma Sūtra, op. cit.,* Introduction, pp. 109 ff.

knowledge."[23] They are received through intuition. This intuitive experience of God or *anubhava* is a reality which does not change. "Intuitions abide while interpretations change."[24] Radhakrishnan also maintains that intuition testifies to an *objective reality.* "To say that God exists means that spiritual experience is attainable. The possibility of this experience is the most conclusive proof of the reality of God."[25]

It must be admitted that it is extremely difficult to get a clear-cut picture of Radhakrishnan's view on this matter. There are several areas of perplexity which are left unclear, and one should guard against mistaking perplexity for profundity. It is possible to raise several questions with regard to the place of intuition in religion, particularly in Hinduism as expounded by Radhakrishnan. One is the relation between *tarka* and *anubhava,* between reason and intuition. Is the latter infallible? What is the place of intellect in religion? What is involved is the whole question of the *validity* or the *truth* of religious experience itself. There are statements in Radhakrishnan where he maintains that intuition is infallible. It is direct, immediate, and complete—*ātma sākṣikam anutpannam.* In other places he says that intuitive experience needs the philosophic criticism of reason to justify its validity. "Simply because the deliverances of intuition appear incontestable to the seer or happen to be shared by many, it does not follow that they are true. Subjective certitude, where validity consists in mere inability to doubt, is different from logical certainty."[26] Intuitive experience has certitude, but lacks con-

---

23 *An Idealist View of Life, op. cit.,* p. 154.
24 *Ibid.,* p. 90.
25 Quoted in *The Philosophy of Sarvepalli Radhakrishnan, op. cit.,* p. 409.
26 *Contemporary Indian Philosophy, op. cit.,* p. 270.

ceptual clearness. *Tarka* helps to give conceptual clarity to experience. The relation between reason and intuition is that between the part and the whole. Intellectual knowledge is not false, it is partial, fragmentary, inadequate. Intellect by itself cannot give knowledge of reality, but it can help to clarify and validate the experience of religion. Intuition, according to Radhakrishnan, is "integral experience" and as such, it is beyond reason, though not against reason. "As it is the response of the whole man to reality, it involves the activity of reason also."[27] Radhakrishnan argues that although the religious view of reality has to be harmonized with the scientific account of the universe, religion should not be subordinated to science.

The second question is concerned with the relativity of religious experiences. Radhakrishnan refers to the experiences of the mystics in different countries, who profess different religions. Now, although there are obvious similarities in the form of their mystic experience and the ways in which they try to describe their joy—and to these Radhakrishnan draws pointed attention—it is equally obvious that the content of the religious values apprehended by them is often different. Thus the content of the experiences of Ramakrishna Paramahamsa is different from that of St. Theresa.[28] In such cases how does one determine the truth of one experience as against the other? Or should one accept all as valid, even those which might be incompatible with one another? The criteria of judgment are not there and, in any case, it is the individual subject who has to use his *tarka* to evaluate the different experiences. Radhakrishnan follows the line of Sankara when he distin-

27 *Ibid.*, p. 269.

28 For a discussion about Experience and Interpretation see *The Brahma Sūtra, op. cit.*, Introduction, pp. 114 ff.

guishes the contemplation of the Absolute and the worship of the personal God, maintaining that there is no contradiction between the two. But although he maintains that rationalist logic and mystic contemplation need not contradict each other, he does not make clear why, when all is said and done, contemplation of the Absolute and the resultant experience of unity alone is considered higher than personalist *bhakti*. This leads to another question that might be raised in this context, namely, the object of *anubhava*. What is it that is experienced? If it is the Supreme Reality and if the intuitive experience is one of unity, who is the subject of the experience? It is not merely an epistemological question but also a metaphysical one, involving the relation between God and man. This is also the question which Ramanuja raised against Sankara in another form, and it has rightly been pointed out that the question is still to be answered.

In spite of these observations, it must be said that by drawing attention to the place of *anubhava* in religion, Radhakrishnan has tried to bridge the gulf between mystic and prophetic religion. The contrast between the two has been unnecessarily overemphasized. There is considerable force in Paul Tillich's argument that mysticism need not contradict, but may intensify, prophetic religion. In an article evaluating Martin Buber's thought, Tillich emphasizes this point.[29] He shows that whereas Roman Catholicism has been able to include mysticism in its pattern of religious life, Protestantism, for various reasons, has had a very ambiguous relation to it, being sometimes antimystical and often indifferent to its significance. However, when recognizing the need for a daily encounter of the "I"

---

29 Paul Tillich, *The Theology of Culture* (New York: Oxford University Press, 1959), pp. 192 ff.

with the eternal "Thou" to deepen the meaning of religious life and to strengthen the ethical sense, one should not ignore the dangers involved in standing on the very "brink of being." Radhakrishnan, however, seems to feel that it is religious *anubhava* alone which can provide a basis for reconciling not only *dristi* and *tarka* but also the different religions. To emphasize this he writes:

> When the Upanishads speak of *jnāna* or *gnosis,* when the Buddha speaks of *bodhi* or enlightenment, when Jesus speaks of the truth that will make us free, they refer to the mode of direct spiritual apprehension of the Supreme, in which the gap between truth and Being is closed. Their religion rests on the testimony of the Holy Spirit, on personal experience, on mysticism as defined by St. Thomas Aquinas, *cognitio dei experimentalis.* From the affirmations of spiritual experience, we find that it is possible to reconcile the conclusions of logical understanding with the apprehensions of integral insight.[30]

THE SANĀTANA DHARMA

It has been maintained that Radhakrishnan is not only an interpreter of Hinduism, but also a defender of and apologist for the essential values of Vedānta as expounded by the great Sankara. Radhakrishnan belongs to that group of seers and thinkers in modern India, who may rightly be described as *Neo-Vedāntins,* because in their writings, with minor deviations, they follow the general lines laid down by Sankara. It is to these essentials of the Vedānta that Ramakrishna Paramahamsa gave spiritual expression, and Swami Vivekananda theological justification. Radhakrishnan has consistently tried to give them a philosophic justification in modern times. Radhakrishnan is loyal to the essential values of *Vedānta;* yet he is not narrowly paro-

---

30 "Fragments," p. 60.

chial about it. Instead of fruitless competition, he calls for genuine co-operation among religions, strongly advocating a fellowship of faiths.

Radhakrishnan repudiates narrow-mindedness and rivalries in the realm of religion. When the world today is moving toward more co-operation and larger unity, religions should not insist on limited vision and narrow loyalties. "A little less missionary ardour, a little enlightened scepticism will do good to us all."[31] Exclusive claims by particular religions have always been a source of pride, fanaticism, and division. It is only the ignorant who show an arrogant dislike of other religions. With greater study of the basic principles of world religions, mankind can steadily move toward informed understanding, larger sympathy, and mutual respect, free from fanaticism and bitterness.

The different religions, according to Radhakrishnan, are only aspects of the one eternal religion. To cling to the historically conditioned forms of religion is to bind oneself to the realm of the relative. It should be to religion, not to religion*s*, that one should give his loyalty. The unchanging substance of religion is "the evolution of man's consciousness." The different religions are merely the expressions of it and are therefore imperfect and relative in their historical forms. The essence and the unity of religions is to be found in that which is divine or universal, not in what is temporary and local. There is no such thing as "a faith delivered once for all to the saints." All religions are part of the same pilgrimage of the human spirit to the Eternal, and the unity of religions is to be found in their spiritual aspiration. He writes in what is now a familiar strain:

---

[31] *Ibid.*, p. 72.

The diversity in the traditional formulations tends to diminish as we climb up the scale of spiritual perfection. All the paths of ascent lead to the same mountain top. This convergent tendency and the remarkable degree of agreement in the witness of those who reach the mountain top are the strongest proof of the truth in religion.[32]

The implications of this and similar statements will be examined at a later stage. But the general line of argument, which Radhakrishnan consistently follows, is clear. What is needed today, according to Radhakrishnan, is not *fusion* but a *fellowship* of faiths, the only basis for which is the *sanātana dharma,* the eternal religion.

---

32 *Ibid.,* p. 77.

3. *God and the World*

THE RELATION BETWEEN GOD AND THE WORLD is one of the most crucial problems in philosophy, because both the meaning of history and the significance of religious life depend upon it. It raises the enquiry regarding the relation between the Absolute, which is the ultimate ground and source of all existence, and the personal God, with whom man can enter into warm, personal communion. For one thing, it is the question of theism and absolutism: is the God of *bhakti,* with whom man can have joyful communion, identical with the Absolute, who is unrelatable? For another, it is also a question of the status of the world of history: is history, with its joys and sorrows, its ambiguities, perplexities, struggles, and achievements, of any value in the sight of God? Implied in all this is the basic question about the relation between metaphysics and ethics in Radhakrishnan's philosophy. Has Radhakrishnan succeeded in interpreting Hinduism as *a view of life,* which can support Hinduism as *a way of life* in the modern world? At a time when the destiny of the individual and the nation is bound up with active participation in history, it is not merely academic interest, but practical need which ought to raise these questions on a deeper level. Radhakrishnan's answer is mainly an exposition and interpretation of Upanishadic thought, in particular of the monistic Vedānta of Sankara. He upholds the unity of God and the Absolute, and so interprets the doctrine of *māyā* as to preserve the reality of the world.

THE PRIMACY OF BEING

As a philosopher, Radhakrishnan rightly emphasizes the primacy of Being as the ground of all existence. Being is the most universal and most comprehensive concept. The very existence of this world implies the existence of Being from which the world derives. Being is the foundation of all existence. "If Being were not, nothing can possibly exist. Being is in all that exists." The nature of Being is unfolded through a study of existence. Following the Upanishads Radhakrishnan maintains that there is only *one* Being and that Being is the Divine *Spirit*. "To say that God exists . . . is to say that God is Being itself." Ultimate Reality is one, not many; it is Spirit, not matter. Radhakrishnan is thus an avowed monist who clearly identifies God and the Absolute. He goes on to say that "this is the concept of the *Brahman* formulated in the Upanishads. It is the 'I am that I am' of the Christian Scripture."[1]

The problem of philosophy has been and still is to relate the conception of Ultimate Reality to the world of becoming. It is to relate the changing, time-conditioned history to the permanent and eternal *Brahman,* without sacrificing the reality of history on the one hand and the absoluteness of the *Brahman* on the other. Radhakrishnan

1 "Fragments," p. 39.

recognizes this problem and tries to work out his answer along the lines of Sankara's interpretation. *Brahman* is both *nirguṇa* (without qualities) and *saguṇa* (with qualities). As pure being, *Brahman* cannot be described. At best one can say what the *Brahman* is not, not what it is. When asked to define the nature of the *Brahman,* the seer of the Upanishad sat silent and when pressed for an answer exclaimed that the *Brahman* is silence.[2] But Radhakrishnan rightly argues that it is a misunderstanding of Sankara to conclude that merely because he claims that *Brahman* cannot be described, to him *Brahman* is therefore a negative concept, "a mere indeterminate blank, an uncomfortable night of nothing," *Brahman* is "not a mystery hidden in a cloud of negative phrases."[3] A negative description does not deprive the *Brahman* of its positive meaning; because a negation is only an affirmation of absence, and the negative has meaning only in relation to the positive. That is why the Upanishads while talking about the *Brahman* say *neti, neti* (not this, not this), but describe the *Brahman* as *sat-chit-ānanda* (truth-consciousness-bliss).

However, *nirguṇa Brahman* and *saguṇa Brahman* are not two entities, but one and the same, viewed from different points of view. *Nirguṇa* is Being-in-repose, *Saguṇa* is Being-in-activity. The transition from one to the other is through divine freedom. Pure Being is not locked up in its own transcendence. It is this concept of divine freedom in activity that unites the static and dynamic nature of Being. This also helps one to understand the conception of creation as to how or why the world owes its existence to God. He writes:

---

2 *The Hindu View of Life, op. cit.,* p. 26.
3 *The Brahma Sūtra, op. cit.,* Introduction, p. 126.

The Supreme has necessary being, or more accurately, it is its own being (*svayambhu*) and it is infinite because it possesses infinite possibilities. The mystery of the world abides in freedom. Freedom is the primordial source and condition of all existence. It precedes all determination.[4]

This statement has several implications. First, that Being is not just static, but dynamic, that repose does not rule out activity. Second, that freedom implies both potentiality and actuality, so that the existence of possibilities within the Godhead and the actualization of one particular possibility are both based on divine freedom. Third, it means that creation is the fruit of the divine exercise of freedom and the world exists because of the sustaining presence and activity of God. Creation, says Radhakrishnan, is "the will of God."

The cosmic side of Being is *Īśvara* who is the *Brahman,* active in his freedom as Lord and Creator. He is the mediating principle between the *Brahman* and the world, relating "the timeless calm and peace and the timeful joy of activity." In the *Brahman* there are infinite possibilities, because absolute being is also absolute freedom. One of these possibilities is being translated into the world of time and space through *Īśvara*. Therefore the world is a manifestation of one specific possibility of the *Brahman.* As to why this particular possibility came into existence, Radhakrishnan says that it is a mystery, simply an expression of divine freedom. The word *Brahman* is derived from the word *"brih"* meaning "to grow." It is the nature of the *Brahman* to grow into the world. The world is an affirmation of the Absolute. The universe is the energizing of God.[5] It is *līlā* or free play, like the work of an artist

4 "Fragments," p. 40.

5 *The Reign of Religion in Contemporary Philosophy* (London: Macmillan & Co., Ltd., 1920), p. 443.

whose creations are the worlds.[6] To avoid any kind of dualism between the *Brahman* and *Īśvara,* Rhadakrishnan points out that "while the Absolute (*Brahman*) is the transcendent divine, God (*Īśvara*) is the cosmic divine. While the Absolute is total reality, God is the Absolute from the cosmic end."[7] Religious experience gets its meaning and reality through its contact with the personal God. He says,

In religious experience personal encounter is as real as the encounter of subject and object in cognitive experience. We meet a "thou" whom we can influence by prayer and worship. While Brahman is the transpersonal ground and abyss of everything, Īśvara is the Personal God. Brahman is the object of *nirvikalpa samādhi,* Īśvara is the object of *savikalpa samādhi.*[8]

Radhakrishnan compares the relation between *Brahman* and *Īśvara* to the relation between God and the *logos* in St. John's Gospel. The "world relatedness" of God is brought out through the conception of *Īśvara* or the *logos.* However, the created world does not in any way affect the *Brahman.* It makes no difference, it cannot add or take away anything from the *Brahman.* "All the sources of its being are found within itself. The world of change does not disturb the perfection of the Absolute."[9]

MAJOR POINTS IN RADHAKRISHNAN'S SYSTEM

At the risk of oversimplification and perhaps some repetition it might be helpful to draw attention to some of the major points in the metaphysics of Radhakrishnan. Charles

6 *Contemporary Indian Philosophy, op. cit.,* p. 286.
7 *Ibid.,* p. 281.
8 *The Brahma Sūtra, op. cit.,* Introduction, p. 126.
9 *Contemporary Indian Philosophy, op. cit.,* p. 285.

A. Moore singles out several points in the structure of Radhakrishnan's metaphysical system.[10] Some of these are relevant in this context.

• Ultimate Reality—the *Brahman*—is One, and therefore plurality is only an appearance. There are numerous statements in Radhakrishnan to say that this "appearance" is not a dream nor an illusion, but one should not forget that Radhakrishnan's position is *advaita*—absolute monism.

• Ultimate Reality is spiritual. This is the position of absolute idealism, by upholding which, Radhakrishnan rejects all materialistic views of reality as inadequate, partial, and misleading.

• The *Brahman* has two aspects: *nirguṇa,* the impersonal, indescribable Absolute and *saguṇa,* the personal and qualitatively describable God. The impersonality of the *Brahman* does not mean that it is purely a negative concept. It simply means that it exceeds both the mere finite and the infinite. The fullness of being transcends all categories. It is the "totally other." This negative account does not deprive the *Brahman* of its positive being, for "the inexhaustible positivity" of *Brahman* bursts through all conceptual forms.

• The existence of this world of name and form and the meaning of history are a mystery, which is expressed in terms of the doctrine of *māyā*. This does not mean that the world is illusory, but only that it has a nonultimate or dependent status. This point has to be considered in greater detail in the next section.

• *Brahman* is indescribable in the sense that human conceptual forms cannot exhaust it, but it is in some way characterized by value. *Brahman* is not only being and

---

10 *The Philosophy of Sarvepalli Radhakrishnan, op. cit.,* pp. 298 ff.

freedom, but also *sat-chit-ānanda.* This is a point which has important implications for ethics, and Radhakrishnan strongly repudiates any suggestion that the Vedāntic view of Reality does not make room for moral action. Quoting the Upanishads Radhakrishnan says, "God is both truth and virtue."[11]

Moore is of the opinion that Radhakrishnan's metaphysics provides a solid ground for his ethics, that the Hindu way of life thus has the foundation of the Hindu view of life as expounded by Radhakrishnan. It justifies *moksha* as the ultimate spiritual goal and the doctrines of *karma* and rebirth as providing the means for orderly, spiritual progress. Ethics becomes an indispensable aid in achieving *moksha.* Morality, though ultimately transcended, provides opportunities for man for spiritual advancement and eventual perfection. However, two critical observations have to be made here. One is that in the discussion on God and the Absolute, in many of his books, Radhakrishnan leaves several perplexities unclarified. Sometimes he speaks of *saguṇa* and *nirguṇa, Īśvara* and the *Brahman,* suggesting a twofold distinction in Ultimate Reality. In other places he points out that there is a fourfold distinction of the Supreme Being—*Brahman, Īśvara, Hiraṇyagarbha* or the World Spirit in its subtle form, and *Virāj,* the World Spirit in its gross form.[12] These are said to bring out the aspects of the Supreme. At other times he maintains that these are logical distinctions only, the Supreme itself being a unity. A further indication of the *Brahman's* relation to the world is given by saying that the World Spirit creates, sustains, and ultimately resolves

11 Brihadāraṇyaka ii, 5, 11 cited in *Eastern Religions and Western Thought, op. cit.,* p. 104.

12 See "Fragments," pp. 40, 41 ff.

the universe, the three aspects brought out by the well-known Hindu trinity—Brahma, Viṣṇu, and Śiva. Moreover, the use of the Aristotelian concept of the *actus purus* and the Johannine concept of the *logos* often makes this discussion even more perplexing. One has to raise the question whether Radhakrishnan's *Īśvara* is the equivalent of the Johannine *logos* from the point of view of metaphysics; for the God of whom St. John talks in his prologue, is surely not the impersonal Absolute, but God the Father. Therefore the comparison breaks down at the very point which it is supposed to clarify.

The other question, as Webb points out, has deeper implications.[13] In spite of Radhakrishnan's efforts to point out that *Īśvara,* the personal God, is equally important, it is unquestionably true that to Radhakrishnan, personality is a transient phenomenon, or at best a concession belonging to the lower level. To him absolutism is intrinsically superior to theism; and, as a result of this attitude, Hinduism, though making room for devotion to a personal God, certainly regards the quest for the *Brahman* as the highest form of piety. Therefore, in spite of Radhakrishnan's vehement insistence on the need for devotion, the importance of ethics, and the reality of the world, the shadow of absolutism seems to hang over all that he says in this respect.

THE DOCTRINE OF MĀYĀ AND THE STATUS OF THE WORLD

The question of the status of the world is bound up with the interpretation of the doctrine of *māyā,* about which there is a good deal of ignorance and misunderstanding. The world in Hindu thought is often said to be a perpe-

[13] *The Philosophy of Sarvepalli Radhakrishnan, op. cit.,* p. 385.

tual procession of events in which nothing permanently abides.[14] The Hindu and the Buddhist systems accept the fact of *samsāra,* what Plato describes as "the world of coming to be and passing away." Before one can raise the question about the meaning of this world and the purpose of human life in it, it is necessary to understand the nature of the world itself. Is human life an accident in a blind impersonal process, or is it a purposeful creation destined to achieve a goal? In the world where everything is subject to change, what is permanent and what is transient? These are some of the questions which have to be considered carefully.

The Sanskrit word *sristi,* usually translated by "creation," Radhakrishnan points out, literally means "emanation, letting loose."[15] The world is the self-manifestation of the creative energy of God. The world then is dependent upon the *Brahman.* In other words, whereas *Brahman* alone is the absolute, independent Reality, all the rest is relative and dependent. Plato's answer to this question was that the empirical world is between being and nonbeing, that it is not an illusion, but that neither is it ultimate. This, maintains Radhakrishnan, is the view of Sankara also. He argues that it is a distortion of Sankara's doctrine of *māyā* to say that the world is an illusion, without meaning and significance. One must note that Indian thinkers like Sri Aurobindo on the contrary claim that to Sankara the world is an illusion. But Radhakrishnan strongly defends Sankara on this score. His own interpretation is so bound up with the defense and exposition of Sankara, that it is difficult to see where Sankara's thought ends and Radhakrishnan's

14 *The Brahma Sūtra, op. cit.,* Introduction, pp. 135 ff. For a scholarly and comprehensive treatment of the doctrine of *Māyā,* see P. D. Devanandan, *The Concept of Māyā* (London: Lutterworth Press, 1950).

15 *Ibid.,* p. 140.

begins. Radhakrishnan says that although in the history of Hindu thought, many have misunderstood Sankara's doctrine of *māyā* as illusionism, Sankara himself never claimed that this world is unreal. Radhakrishnan observes:

Sankara, who is rightly credited with the systematic formulation of the doctrine of *māyā,* tells us that the highest reality is unchangeable, and therefore that changing existence such as human history has not ultimate reality (*pāramārthika satta*). He warns us, however, against the temptation to regard what is not completely real as utterly illusory. The world has empirical being (*vyāvahārika satta*) which is quite different from illusory existence (*pratibhāsika satta*). Human experience is neither ultimately real nor completely illusory. . . . The world is not a phantom, though it is not (ultimately) real.[16]

It follows that any repudiation of the reality of the world will make all ethical relations meaningless. Therefore, Radhakrishnan examines the whole doctrine of *māyā* and concludes that it does not make the world an illusion, a mirage, a dream. On the contrary, it simply indicates that the world is "relatively real." He states that he has interpreted the doctrine of *māyā* "so as to save the world and give it real meaning."[17] What does the doctrine of *māyā* mean? Several interpretations are possible and not all of them have implications for the status of the world.

• *Māyā* indicates that the world is "derived being." The world is an expression of the Absolute, not the Absolute itself. "To mark the distinction between Absolute Being and dependent being, we call the latter *māyā.*"[18] The world depends on the *Brahman,* but the *Brahman* does not depend on the world. This one-sided dependence

16 *Eastern Religions and Western Thought, op. cit.,* p. 86.
17 "Reply," p. 800.
18 *Ibid.,* p. 800.

of the world on the *Brahman* is illustrated by the familiar similes of mistaking a rope for a snake or shell for silver. The purpose of these analogies, however, is not to suggest that the world is a dream or an illusion, but that the relationship is such that the world exists without any change in the being of the Absolute. "The world is not essential being like the Brahman; nor is it mere non-being. It cannot be defined as either being or non-being."[19] Therefore, the world is described as *māyā,* meaning that its being is dependent or derived being.

• *Māyā* describes the temporal or transitory character of the world. The *Brahman* is eternal, whereas the world is temporal. There was a time when the world was not and there will be a time when it will cease to be. History has a beginning and an end. But this does not mean that the interim period between the beginning and the end is an illusion. "To consider history as transitory is not to equate it with the non-existent or the illusory."[20]

• *Māyā* denotes the "creative power" of the *Brahman,* who as *Īśvara* creates the world. It is pointed out that the word *māyā,* is derived from the root *"ma"* which originally meant "to build or produce forms." "There is no suggestion that the forms, the events and the objects produced by *māyā* or the form-building power of God, the *māyāvin,* are only illusory. . . . The world is not a deception but the occasion for it."[21] The analogy of *līlā,* or play, suggests the free, spontaneous overflow of this form-building power or energy into the universe. "The world is the profoundest expression of the divine nature . . . the analogy (*līlā*) is not intended to suggest that the universe is a meaningless

19 *The Bhagavadgītā, op. cit.,* Introduction, p. 38.
20 "Reply," p. 801.
21 *The Bhagavadgītā, op. cit.,* Introduction, pp. 40 ff.

show made in a jest. The world is created by God out of the abundance of His joy."[22]

• *Māyā* also means *mystery*. Why does the world exist at all? How can Absolute Being be the foundation and source of all empirical existences? Why do particular forms of existence dance on the stillness of pure Being? This question cannot be answered satisfactorily by logical means. One can say only that "it is a mystery, *māyā*." How can there be self-limitation in the *Brahman* in creating the world? "From where we are we can only say that it is a mystery (*māyā*) or is the divine will. . . ."[23] This use of the term *māyā* obviously does not in any way affect the status of the world.

• *Māyā* is also used to point out "the dual character of the world process."[24] Radhakrishnan points out that in the world process, there is the Divine interacting with primal matter (*purusha* and *prakriti*). This duality between the Divine and the primal matter is the means for the gradual unfolding of the Divine and continues from the initial creation till the final consummation of the world. This dual character of the world process is also sometimes indicated by the word *māyā*.

• *Māyā* also refers to ignorance—*avidyā*—by which the real nature of the world is hidden from man. "This non-knowing is *avidyā*. It is also different from the real and the unreal. If it attains either reality or collapse into nothingness, there would be no tension, no process. So the world is said to be *sad-asad-vilaksaṇa,* different from the real and

---

22 *Eastern Religions and Western Thought, op. cit.*, pp. 92 ff. See also *The Hindu View of Life, op. cit.*, p. 69; *An Idealist View of Life, op. cit.*, p. 344.

23 *Religion and Society* (London: Allen & Unwin, Ltd., 1942), p. 104.

24 "Reply," p. 801.

the unreal."[25] This *avidyā* must therefore be avoided because it misleads one to accept as ultimate that which is only relative.

> The view which regards multiplicity as ultimate is deceptive (māyā), for it causes the desire to live separate and independent lives. . . . It tempts us to accept as real bubbles which will be broken, cobwebs which will be swept away.[26]

The relevant interpretation of the doctrine of *māyā* is therefore of great significance to a responsible understanding of the status of the world. A proper understanding of Sankara's interpretation of the Upanishads will not lead one to reject the world, but to give it that value which is its due and nothing more. It helps one to take the world seriously, but not too seriously as final and ultimate. *Brahman* alone is ultimate Reality, the world is "relatively real," it is not an illusion or an empty dream. Radhakrishnan goes on to remark:

> When the Hindu thinkers ask us to free ourselves from *māyā*, they are asking us to shake off our bondage to the unreal values which dominate us. They do not ask us to treat life as an illusion or be indifferent to the world's welfare.[27]

The question whether Radhakrishnan's interpretation of *māyā* is faithful to the classical values of Hinduism is sometimes raised by scholars who criticize him for apparently deviating from the ancient lines. Such criticisms are both unnecessary and unhelpful, for they fail to do justice to the larger purpose of Radhakrishnan. It should be noted that even among the classical exponents of the Vedānta there are strong differences of opinion on points of interpretation. The various commentaries on the *prasthāna*

---

25 "Reply," pp. 801–802.
26 *Eastern Religions and Western Thought, op. cit.*, p. 94 f.
27 *Ibid.*, p. 47.

traya—the triple basis of Vedānta, namely, the *Upanishads*, the *Brahma Sūtra*, and the *Bhagavadgītā*,—although agreeing on certain fundamentals, differ in points of view and interpretation. Radhakrishnan himself has now completed his trilogy of commentaries on these three sacred books, giving long introductory expositions and detailed exegesis. Why should one deny him his right to interpret these books on the basis of his experience and authority? What is important today in India is not so much the question of fidelity to past forms of Hindu thought, as meaningfulness and relevance to the needs of the present.

A more important question with regard to Radhakrishnan's interpretation of *māyā* and the resultant doctrine of the world is whether it can sustain a meaningful view of history and a responsible sense of ethical values. A brief review of some of the points of criticism and Radhakrishnan's answers has already been made. At this point however, the question has to be put more insistently. Can a doctrine of creation, *srisṭi*, understood as an emanation, a cutting loose, that is, a doctrine which does not involve the willful purpose of God, but only a spontaneous process, sustain, guard and fulfill the values of history? Admitting that the world is dependent on God, does the conception of the world as "relatively real" provide incentive and opportunity for man to pursue values like truth, goodness, justice, and beauty in the drama of history? How can God redeem the world without himself getting involved in both the suffering and the healing process in the world? The implications of these questions for the nature and destiny of man in history, have to be worked out more fully than has been done so far in Radhakrishnan's interpretation of *māyā*, if the connection between the Hindu view of life and the Hindu way of life today has to be established on a more firm metaphysical basis.

4. *Man and Society*

RADHAKRISHNAN'S TEACHING ON THE NATURE and destiny of man and the structure of society follows the general pattern of classical Hinduism. There are, however, changes of emphasis within that pattern. The major sources for his teachings in this respect are the two chapters on Hindu Dharma in *The Hindu View of Life,* the chapter on "The Individual and the Social Order in Hinduism" in *Eastern Religions and Western Thought,* and his Kamala lectures published under the significant title *Religion and Society.* Sections in the introductions to the *Bhagavadgītā* and the more recent *Brahma Sūtra* also deal with the doctrine of man, *karma,* and freedom, and the conception of the goal for the individual and society. There is a subtle shift of emphasis from self to personality. *Karma* is interpreted more as a principle of continuity than as a retributive rule of life. The body is not a hindrance, a downward drag to be discarded, but an instrument for the fulfillment of *dharma.* In the social order, according to Radhakrishnan, the principle of caste is admitted, but is determined not on the basis of birth (*jāti*), but on one's intrinsic quality (*guṇa*). It will be of help to deal briefly with the classical ideal as interpreted by Radhakrishnan before considering some of the issues involved in his conception of man and society.

THE NATURE AND DESTINY OF MAN

The Hindu understanding of individual life and its relation to society is based on three strands which constitute the fabric of Hindu social order:[1] (a) the fourfold object of individual life—the *purushārtha,* which defines the goals one should pursue; (b) the fourfold succession of the stages of life—the *āshrama dharma,* which indicates the various kinds of duties one should perform in the different periods of one's life; and (c) the fourfold order of society—the *varṇa dharma,* which lays down the duties of the different castes. Radhakrishnan points out that this tested pattern was designed as a way of progressive training for the individual, who ought to pursue not only one's own immediate gain, but also the larger good of society. These are well-known ideals, and only a few words need be said about them.

The four ends of individual life are the following: *dharma, artha, kāma* and *moksha. Dharma* from the root "dhr" is that which sustains or supports, and is related to the Rig Vedic conception of *rita,* the cosmic and moral order to which both gods and men were subject. It is the principle which gives order, coherence, and direction to the different activities of life. "It is not a religious creed or cult imposing an ethical or social rule. It is the complete rule of life, the harmony of the whole man who finds a right and just law of his living."[2] An individual fulfills

---

1 *Eastern Religions and Western Thought,* pp. 351 ff.

2 *Ibid.,* p. 353.

the law of his being by performing his appointed *dharma*. *Artha* stands for wealth or material well-being. Radhakrishnan correctly maintains that poverty was never a national ideal in India, glorified for its own sake, and that classical Hinduism had a balanced view of wealth. Although it is not an end in itself, material welfare has a place in the total life of the individual and society. *Kāma* literally means desire. It stands for the normal enjoyment of life, not its excess, referring to the emotional being of man, his desires and appetites, to which due recognition should be given. *Moksha,* salvation or release, is the final end. It is the chief goal and destiny of man. *Moksha* is simply freedom in the highest sense.

> To inquire into his true self, to live in and from it, to determine by its own energy what it shall be inwardly and what it shall make of its outward circumstances, to found the whole life on the power and truth of spirit, is *moksha* or spiritual freedom.[3]

These four ends, says Radhakrishnan, are designed to satisfy the different sides of human nature—the ethical, the economic, the emotional, and the spiritual. He points out, however, that man's true greatness consists in moving on to the universality of spiritual freedom which is *moksha* and that the other three are subordinate to this.

The *āshrama dharma* lays down certain duties which are in accordance with the needs and possibilities of the four stages in the life of an individual. There is first the young student or *brhamchārin.* His *dharma* is not merely to gather knowledge, but to acquire the discipline of spiritual wisdom under the guidance of a teacher. The duty of the householder or *grihasta* is to maintain and ensure as a so-

---

[3] *Ibid.,* p. 352.

cial responsibility the continuity of the family. Hinduism does not unnecessarily glorify the unmarried state. It is possible to move on to higher life through the normal way of living in the world. When the children are settled and one's social responsibilities are fulfilled, the next stage is that of the forest dweller or *vānaprastha.* He is called upon to retire from active life, to be away from the busy strife of the world, so that he can lead a life of meditation. The *monk* or the *sannyāsin* is one who has renounced all. This is the last stage, the supreme ideal, and Hinduism has always given the highest respect to that person who has renounced all and has therefore attained spiritual freedom. The ideal man of India, says Radhakrishnan, is not the magnanimous man of Greece or the valiant knight of mediaeval Europe, but the true *sannyāsin,* who, like the Swan (*hamsa*), is equally free on land or water, or in the sky. Some of his characteristics are as follows:

> A freedom and fearlessness of spirit, an immensity of courage, which no defeat or obstacle can touch, a faith in the power that works in the universe, a love that lavishes itself without demand of return and makes life a free servitude to the universal spirit, are the signs of the perfected man.[4]

India, says Radhakrishnan, has clung fast to this ideal at all times, from the seers of the Upanishads and the Buddha to Ramakrishna and Gandhi. This is true today also; for, in India, even in this atomic age, the man who is most respected is not the politician or the scientist, but the saint and the *sannyāsin* who, though they are in the world, are not attached to it but claim to have attained freedom of the spirit.

The conception of individual life and destiny with its

---

[4] *Ibid.,* p. 380.

clear-cut goals and smooth transition from one stage to another has always been very familiar in India, but one cannot be sure whether it was universally adhered to by all people at all times. At best it has remained an ideal to be approximated, not a rule that was strictly followed. But such a time-honored ideal, advocated by the great law giver of India, Manu, implies a certain understanding of man, his nature, duty, and destiny. It means that both the purpose of life and the power to fulfill that purpose are to be found in man himself. Man has within himself both the possibility and the resources to attain his true being. This freedom of the spirit, however, is limited on the one hand by the doctrine of *karma-samsāra* and on the other by the hierarchy of the caste structure. Nevertheless, in spite of these limitations, the necessity and the possibility of man's attaining *moksha* through his efforts, however long the process might be, was not questioned. Some of the major aspects of this individual and social ideal are being reinterpreted today and a restated Hindu doctrine of man is in the making. Radhakrishnan's contribution to this restatement is particularly significant.

FROM SELF TO PERSONALITY

In contemporary India, where there is a search for national unity, political stability, and material well-being, and where the need for social justice is imperative, there is also a persistent questioning about the nature and destiny of man. When so much attention is being paid to the physical well-being of man, the relation of the body to the spirit cannot be ignored. With community development schemes marching ahead, a merely individualistic conception of salvation will fall short of the need for the larger good. In an industrial India, with the inevitable movement of people from one place to another and the shifting from one occupation to another, a rigid, hierarchical caste system cannot provide the necessary mobility and sense of social responsibility. In reinterpreting some of the major doctrines of classical Hinduism, as they touch man and society, Radhakrishnan takes these factors into account. No responsible scholar would venture to suggest that there is *a* Hindu doctrine of man. In the long history of Hinduism and its varied expressions, it will be futile to search for a universally accepted conception of man. Nevertheless, some of its major aspects, which are being reinterpreted at the present time, need briefly to be considered.

The question of the relation between body and spirit has always been a complex one. Classical Hinduism has often maintained that the flesh is the prison house of the spirit and that therefore the body with its desires has to be disciplined and ultimately discarded, so that the spirit may soar to the heights of freedom. Radhakrishnan certainly departs from this view. To him man is essentially spiritual. But, in insisting on the spiritual nature of man, Radhakrishnan is careful not to ignore the fact that he is a creature of this world as well. Man is a "complex, multidimensional being including within him different elements of matter, life, consciousness, intelligence and the divine spark."[5] There need not be any conflict between the desires of the body and the aspirations of the spirit. There should be no one-sided emphasis on either the body or the spirit. "Asceticism is an excess indulged in by those who exaggerate the transcendent aspect of reality."[6] Mar-

5 *The Bhagavadgītā, op. cit.,* Introduction, p. 46.

6 *An Idealist View of Life, op. cit.,* p. 115. See also *The Hindu View of Life, op. cit.,* Chapter III.

riage is not a concession to human weakness, it is a means of spiritual growth. There is nothing unwholesome about sex life. The fact that Siva is sometimes represented as *ardha-nārīśvara* (half-woman-lord) signifies "the co-operative, inter-dependent, separately incomplete but jointly complete masculine and feminine functions of the supreme being." To divide man into body and spirit, to separate the realm of life from the realm of the spirit, therefore, is to violate the integrity of human personality. The body is "the temple of the Holy Spirit"; it is *dharma sādhanam,* the instrument to perform one's rightful duties.[7]

This shift of emphasis from self to personality, and the consequent value placed on the body is also supported by Radhakrishnan with reference to the doctrine of rebirth—*punarjanma.* He remarks:

> The body is a necessity for the soul. A system which believes in rebirth cannot despise bodily life, for every soul has need of it. Personal life is not to be repressed in order to gain the end of religion. It is to be recreated and purified in the light of the higher truth.[8]

Since man is a unity, and life is a continuous series, the body is essential for rebirth. "Rebirth is not an eternal recurrence leading nowhere, but a movement . . . to a future kingdom of God. The soul is constantly performing the miracle of self-embodiment which is a means for self-renewal, a growth into light."[9] This stress on the importance of the body and so on the legitimate need for the material welfare of human beings is one of the most signifi-

---

[7] "Fragments," p. 30.

[8] *Eastern Religions and Western Thought, op. cit.,* p. 32.

[9] *The Brahma Sūtra, op. cit.,* Introduction, p. 193; for a discussion on Rebirth and the possible objections to it, see pp. 198 ff.

cant contributions of Radhakrishnan to the making of a modern Hindu doctrine of man.

"KARMA" AND FREEDOM

When considering man as an ethical individual having social responsibilities in history, the influence of the classical doctrine of *karma* cannot be ignored. In giving a modern interpretation to this doctrine, Radhakrishnan attempts to reconcile the seemingly inexorable operation of the *kārmic* law on the one hand and the freedom of the individual to choose, to decide and act, on the other. According to him the law of *karma* has two sides: one stresses the determinist aspect, and the other emphasizes the free-will aspect.

The determinist side of *karma* is seen in the lawfulness of nature and also in the persistent effects of past actions on the character of the individual. Since biologically man is subject to physical laws, his nature is determined to some extent. But the kind of necessity to which man is subject, is different from the purely mechanical operation of physical laws. "Karma is the impulse out of which life's forms issue. The whole cosmic evolution is called karma. The Supreme undertakes it and there is no reason why the individual *jīva* should not take part in it."[10] However, it must be noted that *karma* "is not a mechanical principle but a spiritual necessity. It is the embodiment of the word and will of God."[11] Because it is derived from God himself, there is a certain inexorableness in its operation. Because God is both the source and the sustainer of the law of *karma* and because God is just, He will not suspend its operation for the sake of particular individuals. This in-

10 *The Bhagavadgītā, op. cit.*, VIII, 3, p. 227.
11 *The Hindu View of Life, op. cit.*, p. 72.

exorable justice in the working out of *karma* is strongly emphasized by Radhakrishnan when he observes:

> If we fall into error no supernatural deliverer will come to our rescue. There is no forgiveness for a broken law. No single word can be unspoken, no single step retracted. The past is determined, however free the future may be.[12]

The retributive aspect of the *kārmic* law simply stresses the principle that whatever a man sows, that he shall reap, that all actions produce their effects without fail, but Radhakrishnan is also concerned with *karma* as a law of continuity. "Karma should be understood not so much as a principle of retribution as one of continuity."[13] He points out that in the past there has been an overemphasis on that aspect of *Karma* which ensured that the results of actions will not go without fruits. Equally important, however, is the other aspect which ensures the continuity of human motivation and effort.

Karma has often been interpreted as fatalistic, inspiring an attitude which resigns itself to the tragedies of life without fighting to change the circumstances. Radhakrishnan, however, does not believe that *karma* destroys man's freedom of will. He disagrees with some of the modern psychologists who tend to regard freedom of will as an "egoistic delusion." According to Radhakrishnan, *Karma* undoubtedly influences a man's actions, but surely does not cancel his freedom to act. "Karma is a condition, not a destiny."[14] To recognize the limitations of man, is not to make him a slave to the circumstances of his birth. Elaborating this point he writes:

---

12 *Kalki* (London: Kegan Paul, 1929), p. 58.

13 *An Idealist View of Life, op. cit.*, p. 275.

14 *The Bhagavadgītā, op. cit.*, p. 48.

While it [the law of *karma*] regards the past as determined, it allows that the future is only conditioned. The spiritual element in man allows him freedom within the limits of his nature. Man is not a mere mechanism of instincts. The spirit in him can triumph over the automatic forces that try to enslave him.[15]

This statement, however, tends to stress the spiritual freedom of man which enables him to rise above the flux of history, rather than the personal freedom that enables him to decide and act in the historic structure of society. But Radhakrishnan wishes not so much to emphasize the reality of freedom as to point out the balance between freedom and necessity in human life. Man should not be a fatalist, because he is "not a plaything of fate or the driftwood on the tide of controlled events. He can actively mould the future instead of passively suffering for the past."[16]

The way of responsible action advocated by Radhakrishnan is well worked out in his commentary on the *Bhagavadgītā*. To Arjuna, who represents man, and who, caught in the struggle of life, attempts to seek refuge in inaction, Krishna teaches the doctrine of *"nishkāma karma"*—action without desire. He demands not the renunciation of work as such, but that of attachment to motives and fruits of action. Man has to accept the given elements in the historical context in which he finds himself. His acceptance, however, should be combined with a spirit of adventure, for "mere acceptance without adventure, mere adjustment without alteration may mean perfection of a kind, peace of a sort, but it is not the perfection of a human being or the peace of a spiritual nature."[17] Thus with regard to the

15 *The Hindu View of Life, op. cit.,* p. 75.
16 *An Idealist View of Life, op. cit.,* p. 279.
17 *Kalki, op. cit.,* p. 66.

individual's ethical responsibility in history, Radhakrishnan so interprets the doctrine of *karma* as to give a balanced emphasis on both the circumstances which limit man and the freedom which enables him to act responsibly. He summarizes his teaching in the following words:

> Life is like a game of bridge. The cards in the game are given to us. We do not select them. They are traced to past *karma* but we are free to make any call as we think fit and lead any suit. Only we are limited by the rules of the game.[18]

THE IDEAL SOCIETY—CASTE AS CLASS

The social thought of Radhakrishnan is based on his conception of the freedom of the individual and the dignity of human personality. What has been said on the doctrine of *Karma* has a large bearing on this. The individual cannot be treated in isolation. History deals with the personal relationships of human beings in the community where the individual's choice, decision, and act have consequences not only for the individual concerned but also for society at large. Hindu social thought has determined the place of the individual in the community by developing the caste system to which religious sanction was given in the course of time. Even political rights and duties were determined by the caste structure, in which both the *rāja-dharma,* the duty of the king, and *prajā-dharma,* the duty of the governed, were laid down according to certain principles. A. R. Wadia correctly observes that there are three major strands in the fabric of Radhakrishnan's treatment of caste.[19] In his *Hindu View of Life* (1926), he was primarily concerned with a defense of Hinduism and so he presented

---

[18] *An Idealist View of Life, op. cit.,* p. 279.

[19] *The Philosophy of Sarvepalli Radhakrishnan, op. cit.,* pp. 766 ff. Wadia's article is an excellent summary of Radhakrishnan's social thought.

the caste system as a social achievement of the Hindus, in spite of its obvious perversions. In *Eastern Religions and Western Thought* (1939), he justifies the principle of the caste system, interpreting it in terms of class, rather than particular castes. In *Religion and Society* (1947), he strongly criticizes the traditional caste system, calling upon his countrymen to change it. In this book there is a renewed emphasis on the freedom and dignity of the individual and a strong criticism of both the rigidity of the caste system and the coercive philosophy of communism.

According to Radhakrishnan, the fourfold division of society, to which the earliest reference is to be found in the *Rig Veda*,[20] is a healthy arrangement based on the character and function of different individuals in society. It was designed to promote the free development of the individual and the healthy growth of society. The *Brahmin* represents spiritual wisdom, the *Kshatriya* stands for executive power, the *Vaiśya* provides skilled production, and the *Śudra* gives devoted service to the society of which they all are integral parts. Radhakrishnan maintains that this fourfold order is meant not just for the Hindus only, but for all mankind, because the man of learning and knowledge, the man of power and action, the skilled craftsman, and the laborer are types of people who are to be found in all countries at all times. Those who are preeminently intellectual are *Brahmins.* Their function is to seek knowledge and to communicate it to others. They engage in the pursuit of truth and give spiritual and moral guidance to the people. "A class of disinterested seekers of truth, supported by society, influencing it, and placed above the corrupting tendency of power, is the very life

---

[20] X, 90.

of social stability and growth."[21] It is the business of the *Kshatriyas* to enforce the principles laid down by the *Brahmins*. The qualities a *Kshatriya* should have are a heroic determination, a dynamic daring, a nobility of soul, and an unflinching resistance to injustice and oppression. Dictatorship, the worship of the State, it is claimed, is alien to the Hindu spirit. Radhakrishnan quotes Rama who tells his brother, "I bear arms for the sake of truth. It is not difficult for me to gain this whole universe, but I desire not even the suzerainty of the heavens if it is to be through unrighteousness."[22] The duty of the *Vaiśyas* is to engage in trade and commerce, without which society cannot lead a normal life. Shrewdness, practical skill, ordered benevolence, ability to make the best use of natural resources, and, to some extent, enlightened self-interest are the marks of this class. *Śudra* represents work and service. Labor is essential to the ordered life of human society; and therefore a sense of the dignity of labor, which is now unfortunately lost, has to be steadily cultivated. Thus the fourfold division of society is functional rather than hereditary; therefore, though rejecting the perversions of the caste system, Radhakrishnan maintains that its basic principle is helpful to the order, stability, and growth of any society.

Strongly advocating the value of this fourfold division based on character and function, Radhakrishnan argues that the whole system is essentially democratic. He offers several reasons for this view.[23] First, it recognizes the spiritual equality of all men. Whatever may be the outward circumstances, each individual is a personality, with the right to grow in his own way. Second, the fourfold

---

21 *Eastern Religions and Western Thought, op. cit.*, p. 358.
22 *Mahabharata,* iii, 134. 3.
23 *Eastern Religions and Western Thought, op. cit.*, pp. 367 ff.

scheme "makes for individuality in the positive sense," because it provides for each individual that type of social duty for which he is best fitted. Third, it emphasizes that all work is "socially useful and from an economic standpoint equally important." Fourth, "the social justice it offers is not a scheme of rights, but of opportunities." This means that the inequalities of men are frankly recognized and that equality is understood not in terms of ability, but in terms of opportunities open to all individuals to contribute to the good of the society. What is beyond the ability of the individual can not be expected of him. "There is no attempt to equalise capacities or level up the requirements." Fifth, the fourfold scheme provides a basis for "true democracy" because it recognizes different kinds of abilities and makes allowance for a proper adjustment and responsible use of different individuals. Instead of mutual rivalry and unhealthy competition, it ensures harmony among spiritual knowledge, political power, economic skill, and physical labor. Sixth, it establishes the important principle that rights and responsibilities go together, that the higher one's place is in the social structure, the greater should be his sense of duty.

Although Radhakrishnan thus maintains the usefulness of the fourfold division, he strongly condemns the caste spirit itself which has prevented the growth of unity among the Hindus. To develop a degree of organic wholeness and a sense of common obligation, the caste spirit must go.[24] About the "sin of untouchability" he writes that what is being done today is "a question not of justice or charity, but of atonement. Even when we have done all that is in our power, we shall not have atoned even for a small frac-

[24] *Religion and Society, op. cit.*, p. 133.

tion of our guilt in this matter."[25] One of his most effective blows to the traditional caste system is his comment on *Bhagavadgītā,* Chapter IV, verse 13, which the orthodox have always upheld as sanctioning the entire structure of the caste system, where Krishna says, "The fourfold order was created by Me according to the divisions of quality and work," interpreting it as divine sanction for the caste divisions according to heredity. In his comment however, Radhakrishnan makes his point quite clear that for him the emphasis in the fourfold order is on *guṇa* (aptitude) and *karma* (work) and not on *jāti* (birth). He goes on to say:

> The fourfold order is designed for human evolution. There is nothing absolute about the caste system which has changed its character in the process of history. . . . The present morbid condition of India broken into castes and subcastes is opposed to the unity taught by the *Gītā,* which stands for an organic as against an atomistic conception of society.[26]

POLITICAL PHILOSOPHY

A brief reference should be made to Radhakrishnan's political thought. He is not a systematic political philosopher, and therefore what he says about some of the issues in this realm has to be gleaned from his writings and speeches made at different times. His approach to political thought is essentially through his philosophy, and his political ideas are naturally influenced by his conception of man and society. Today, as President of the Indian Republic, he is obviously committed to the way of parliamentary democracy, but it should be acknowledged that his commitment to democracy goes much deeper than mere political alignment. To him democracy is a more

---

25 *Ibid.,* pp. 134 ff.

26 *The Bhagavadgītā, op. cit.,* pp. 160–161.

acceptable way of life for man in society than other ways of organized community living. This is so partly because it gives to the individual relatively more freedom to work out his destiny and partly because, according to Radhakrishnan, the religious tradition of India offers a spiritual basis for democracy.

It can be argued, though not always very convincingly, that some of the religious conceptions regarding man and society provide a basis for democracy. It is difficult to maintain that the rule of kings in Indian history was essentially democratic, although most of them were patrons of religion and defenders of their faith. Moreover, today secular humanism is certainly a strong alternative claiming to provide resources for political democracy. In Radhakrishnan's book, *Religion and Society,* there are sections which strongly question the validity of the basis of communism. He points out justifiably that Marx's condemnation of religion as otherworldly is justified only against certain one-sided views of religion, and that communism, in spite of its denial of religious values, has a religious fervor about it.[27] Democracy is based on a recognition of the worth of the individual and a religion like Neo-Vedānta, which upholds the dignity of man by claiming divine status for him, is, it is claimed, a strong support for democracy. Radhakrishnan goes to the extent of saying that "religion includes faith in human brotherhood, and politics is the most effective means of rendering it into visible form. Politics is but applied religion."[28]

But Radhakrishnan's emphasis on democracy is primarily based on the value he places on the worth of indi-

---

27 *Religion and Society,* p. 69 ff.

28 *Education, Politics and War* (Poona, India: International Book Service, 1944), p. 2.

vidual personality, his freedom, and his dignity. "The common man is not common. He is precious, has in him the power to assert his nature against the iron web of necessity."[29] A political structure which recognizes the worth of the individual ought therefore to be supported at all costs. Radhakrishnan goes on to remark that democracy is not just a political arrangement, "but it is the highest religion. The human individual is the highest, the most concrete embodiment of the Spirit on earth and anything which hurts his individuality or damages his dignity is undemocratic and irreligious."[30] Theoretically, this is the place where religion and politics meet in Radhakrishnan.

Liberty is essential to man's moral and spiritual growth, and therefore any form of political compulsion which limits man's liberty cannot be justified. Radhakrishnan criticizes all totalitarian systems which, in the name of the state, attempt to enslave man. He accepts the principle of nonviolence, *ahimsa,* particularly as expounded by Gandhiji, but he makes a distinction between *himsa,* violence, and *danda,* force. *Danda* is one of the traditionally accepted four ways by which kings carried on their administration. Radhakrishnan, though rejecting violence and the gigantic displays of brute power, nevertheless recognizes the need for the proper use of force in political life. "The use of force is permissible when it is ordered in accordance with law by a neutral power in the general interest. . . ."[31]

Radhakrishnan strongly believes in the brotherhood of nations and co-operation among the peoples of the world.

---

29 *Ibid.,* p. 39.

30 *Ibid.,* p. 8.

31 *Mahatma Gandhi, Essays and Reflections on Gandhi's Life and Work,* S. Radhakrishnan, ed. (London: Allen & Unwin, Ltd., First Edition, 1939), p. 357. See also Address to the UNESCO Conference, May 24, 1950.

His support for the United Nations and other international organizations is well known. In a sense this stress on international co-operation is simply another side of his call for a fellowship of faiths. His advocacy of international co-operation is based on his belief that mankind is moving toward a "moral community, a single commonwealth in which the human race will find ordered peace."[32]

SOME ISSUES

This exposition of Radhakrishnan's views on man and society obviously is not exhaustive. But a few critical observations should be made here, drawing attention to certain points. In the first place, when one studies Radhakrishnan's thought on the nature and possibilities of man, one is struck by the relative absence of emphasis on the evil that is seen so glaringly in the life of man and society. There is so much stress on the spirituality of man and consequently on the possibility of his moral goodness, that one gets the impression that to establish the ideal social order all that is necessary is proper effort on the part of individuals. In other words, both the goal and the resources enabling man to reach that goal are to be found within man himself. There is the emphatic teaching that the spirit in man is divine. The question, therefore, arises: From where do evil, selfishness, greed, and exploitation come? It cannot be the spirit, because it is claimed that the spirit in man is essentially divine and therefore good. Whatever be the definition of "evil," can its source be identified so that it can be controlled, defeated, and eradicated? To trace it back to past *karma* would simply raise the same

---

32 *Education, Politics and War, op. cit.,* p. 32. For a larger discussion on Radhakrishnan's political philosophy see Humayun Kabir's article in *The Philosophy of Sarvepalli Radhakrishnan,* pp. 689 ff.

question at another level. To identify it with *avidyā,* ignorance, would raise the question whether, if man had the necessary wisdom, he would have the power to act accordingly. Radhakrishnan himself points out that mere knowledge of ideals, however good they might be, has no power to enable man to reject evil and follow the good. Therefore, this question of the presence and mystery of evil, both in personal life and in the life of society, needs further clarification.

Second, in considering the nature of man, Radhakrishnan lays great stress on man's personality, pointing out that he is a unity of body and spirit. But if *moksha* is understood as "spiritual freedom," how is this unity to be understood in relation to *moksha?* He recognizes the mutual influence of body and spirit in the growth of personality, its failures, and achievements. The question can be raised whether the body is merely *instrumental* to the spirit or whether, at the same time, the relationship has also a *sacramental* character. A close examination of Radhakrishnan's conception of *moksha* gives the impression that in spite of his emphasis on man as a unity of body and spirit, in the last analysis body is something to be left behind. Also, unless *moksha* is interpreted in terms of fulfillment and not just as spiritual freedom, the other three goals of individual life would be secondary and only subservient to the last.

Third, Radhakrishnan's conception of society and his interpretation of caste need further clarification. Although it is true that in the history of Hinduism religious sanction was given to the caste system, is the connection between religion and society so obvious and close as Radhakrishnan seems to make it? To what extent have sociological and economic factors influenced the system? Moreover, can it not be argued, as some responsible scholars point out, that the social structure of the Hindus is primarily secular in character and that therefore social reform need not necessarily wait for religious reform? Further, Radhakrishnan's conception of caste as essentially democratic is difficult to maintain even on the basis of his interpretation, because there is little room for movement from one caste to another. Also, the question should be raised whether the ideal social order, based not on the caste unit, but on the class concept, does full justice to the complexities of modern society. Should not the pervasive influence of evil, manifesting itself in greed, oppression, and exploitation in spite of the best intentions, be given greater recognition in analyzing the social structure of the present and indicating the hope for the future?

5. *The Meaning of History*

UNTIL RECENTLY VERY LITTLE ATTENTION was given to the Hindu understanding of history. This was primarily because of a notion that the Hindu religion was "a-historical" in character and that history was of no significance to the Hindu, therefore. The interpretation of the doctrine of *māyā* simply as "illusion" and the doctrine of *karma* as deterministic resulted in undermining both the status of the world and the freedom of the individual. Although it is true that with the single exception of Kalhana's *Rājatarangiṇi,* classical Hindu literature has hardly any work of importance in the realm of history, it should nevertheless be noted that contemporary Hinduism is very much alive to the importance of history. There is considerable justification for saying that a philosophy of history is in the making in modern India. Some works have already drawn attention to this point.[1] Hinduism can no longer be ac-

[1] See S. J. Samartha, *The Hindu View of History,* Classical and Modern, booklet 36 pp., published by the Christian Institute for the Study of Religion and Society, Bangalore, 1959; P. Sankaranarayanan, *Values in History,* booklet 52 pp., Bharatiya Vidya Bhavan, Bombay, 1962; also B. G. Gokhale, *Indian Thought Through the Ages,* Asia Publishing House, 1961, Chapter I: "Thus It Has Been, The Indian View of History," pp. 1 ff.

cused of being indifferent to history. As a nation, India is no longer a passive spectator of history, but an active participant in its movement, asserting herself increasingly in the affairs of the world. Although it is perhaps too early to seek a full-fledged philosophy of history in contemporary Hinduism, there are indications that a more positive view is slowly emerging.

Radhakrishnan's contribution to the making of a positive view of history in India is of considerable importance. Though there is no systematic treatment of the theme of history as such in Radhakrishnan, nevertheless, his consideration of some of the major doctrines of Hinduism has important consequences for a view of history, as for example his defense of Hinduism against the charges of world negation, his interpretation of the doctrine of *māyā* so as to preserve the reality of the world, and his restatement of the doctrine of *karma* in such a way that the freedom of man is not annulled. These obviously have important implications for his view of history. To him history is a part of the cosmic process, yet has a reality and distinctiveness of its own. Man, as a person, is not only a spectator but also a participant in the drama of history. In the world there is a constant struggle between *dharma* and *adharma,* between good and evil, and man's duty is to co-operate with the good. In this struggle the *avatāras* of God have a special meaning, revealing both the concern of God in the happenings of the world and the possibility of man to attain divine status. The final destiny of the world is *brahma loka,* the kingdom of God. Since God is profoundly concerned with the world of history, one can look forward with confidence and hope to the salvation of all—*sarvamukti.*

HISTORY AND THE COSMIC PROCESS

History is part of the cosmic process which means that between nature, man, and God there is an inseparable continuity. Radhakrishnan shares this view with that of classical Hinduism. His acceptance of the description of the world as *samsāra,* or the world of change, is significant. Indian thinkers, both Hindu and Buddhist, have considered the world as a stream of happenings or a perpetual flow of events. All history is characterized by change and movement. Expressions like "the wheel of time," "the cycle of birth and death," and "the ever-rolling stream," indicate the incessant movement of history. The world, *jagat,* is movement, and it would be dissolved with the cessation of movement.[2] However, the world process "is not an incessant fluctuation comparable to a surging sea. It is a movement with a direction and goal."[3] There is an underlying unity and a definite continuity in the world movement. The primary emphasis is thus on the category of *process,* of which the movement of history is a part.

If the cosmos is thus a process, whence does it proceed and what is its destination? Radhakrishnan follows the Upanishadic affirmation that *Brahman* is that from which everything flows and that into which everything returns in the end. This process has a certain pattern. It proceeds in stages, from matter (*anna*) through life (*prāṇa*), perceptive-instinctive consciousness (*manas*), and reflective consciousness (*Vijnāna*) to spiritual or creative consciousness (*ānanda*).[4] Thus in the cosmic process we have the suc-

---

[2] *An Idealist View of Life, op. cit.,* p. 225.

[3] "Fragments," p. 27.

[4] *Taitt. Upanishad,* iii, 1. See also *Reign of Religion in Contemporary Philosophy,* by S. Radhakrishnan (London: Macmillan & Co., Ltd., 1920), p. 419.

cessive emergence of the material, the organic, the animal, the human, and the spiritual orders. Radhakrishnan works out this theory of evolution, bringing it in relation to modern scientific and philosophic views, particularly to those of Bergson, Lloyd Morgan, Alexander, and Whitehead.[5] However, in this whole process the primacy of the spirit is maintained; for to him "life is a unique kind of activity for which the formulas of matter and energy are not adequate."[6]

Along with continuity, there is also interrelatedness within the world movement. Each event "has an irreducible specificity, a unique itselfness, as also a connection with other events. Each event is just what it is without the influence and assistance of other events."[7] The two striking features in this world of history are continuity and change, connection with the past and creative advance into the future. "Time is connection, not mere succession. . . . Every event has not only a retrospective but prospective reference."[8] History is a progressive manifestation of the values of the spirit. It is the realm in which "the world's unborn soul is struggling to be born."

Although history is not *separate* from the cosmic process it is, however, distinct from nature. The question, what exactly constitutes this distinctiveness, is answered in different ways by different modern thinkers. To Tagore it was to be found in "a change of rhythm," to Aurobindo in the rationality of man. To Radhakrishnan it is to be found in the structure of human personality, in spiritual consciousness. "History is not a branch of biology. The drama of human personalities is distinct from life in the animal

5 "Fragments," pp. 34 ff.

6 *Ibid.*, p. 28.

7 *An Idealist View of Life, op. cit.*, p. 338.

8 *Ibid.*, 239.

kingdom."[9] Because history is part of the cosmic process, human destiny has a longer context and therefore should be considered in the long-range scheme of things. Yet it is recognized that the movement of history cannot be bound by the laws of natural necessity. Radhakrishnan emphasizes this point, saying that "history is neither a chapter of accidents, nor a determined drift. It is a pattern of absolute significance."[10] The precise meaning of such statements as a "determined drift" and "absolute significance" cannot easily be understood and one should, therefore, be careful not to discover unwarranted meaning in some of his statements, but it is obvious that his motive is to establish the reality and significance of history.

VALUES IN HISTORY

A view of history which recognizes that historical events have meaning cannot ignore the question of values—their preservation and possible actualization in the drama of occurrences. It has already been pointed out that for Radhakrishnan, Being is in some way characterized by value. *Sat,* that which is, is also *satyam,* that which is true. Unless the values cherished by men have grounding in the very structure of reality and unless their actualization in the context of human events is somehow guaranteed, history would make little sense. The traditionally accepted triplet of ultimate values—Truth, Goodness, and Beauty have their foundation in God Himself. For Radhakrishnan moral values in history are not just "empirical accidents," but are grounded in reality, "which is the source of the significance of what happens" in the temporal process of

9 "Fragments," p. 29.
10 *Ibid.*, p. 29.

history.[11] Men cannot strive for ideals with courage and conviction unless assured that those ideals are not just accidental fancies but eternal verities which give meaning to life. Emphasizing this point Radhakrishnan writes:

> Moral enthusiasm is possible only if our motive includes the expectation of being able to contribute to the achievement of moral ideals. . . . If ethical thought is profound, it will give a cosmic motive to morality. Moral consciousness must involve a conviction of the reality of ideals.[12]

Granting that eternal values are permanent because they are rooted in Ultimate Reality itself, what then is the possibility of their being actualized in history where evil is a persistent hindrance to their realization and where the temporal structure of time is a constant threat to their permanence? History is the totality of events determined by free persons in the context of society. A historic event is not just a happening, it is an occurrence plus meaning. It is because of the meaningfulness of events that tradition is cherished by mankind and passed on to future generations as a valuable heritage. The meaning of a particular historic event is therefore determined by the value of which it becomes the vehicle. This means that eternal values and temporal history cannot be separated. Values are eternal. They cannot, however, be abstract ideals unrelated to the daily life of man. Moreover, there should be real possibilities of values being actualized in history, enjoyed by people and passed on as a heritage to future generations. To establish political freedom, social justice, religious liberty, and many other values men have strug-

[11] *An Idealist View of Life, op. cit.,* p. 89.
[12] *Eastern Religions and Western Thought, op. cit.,* pp. 81 ff.

gled, fought, and died so that these might become the cherished heritage of future generations.

There are three major problems in connection with the possible actualization of values in history. The first is the importance of individual personality, to assess to what extent man's freedom of will can influence the course of events. This point has been considered, to some extent, in a previous chapter in our discussion of the doctrine of *karma* and its implications. The second is the problem of evil, which, by its persistence in the structures of history, is a hindrance to the realization of values. This will be considered in the next section. The third problem is the question of time which, because of its transitory nature, is a constant threat to the enduring values of history. This is briefly considered here, noting, however, that Radhakrishnan says very little about its implications.

For Radhakrishnan, time has no ultimate significance. It is simply temporality. "The flux of time is a symptom of the disrupted, fallen state of the world. The new heaven and the new earth represent victory over time."[13] Time is empirical, relative, that which comes to be and passes away. The temporal world is the stage in which the souls evolve, but it has no ultimate significance. He writes,

> Time is not all, though the temporal world is the stage on which spiritual values are enacted. The eternal source of spiritual values and the final destiny of all who pursue them is God, the Absolute. Unending history, be it as progress or regress, is the essence of meaninglessness.[14]

Because of the temporal nature of the world, Radhakrishnan does not believe that values can be fully actual-

---

[13] "Reply," p. 799.
[14] *Ibid.*, p. 798.

ized in history. "There is no perfection in the finite. It can only be attained in the infinite. Every actualization in the here and now is but a symbol. . . . The meaning of history is beyond the confines of history."[15] However, Radhakrishnan also believes that progress in history is possible; but whether there are partial fulfillments of value in history, whether these are shadows of, or approximations to, the ultimate values, these are the questions to which no definite answer is given.

EVIL IN HISTORY

A view of history which takes the world seriously and acknowledges man's freedom as a person, confronts the fact of evil. Evil is a threat not only to the possible fulfillment of man's destiny but also to any disclosures of meaning in history. Moreover, it is a persistent hindrance to values being realized in history. In Radhakrishnan's thought there is a tendency to consider evil more in metaphysical than in moral terms and to relegate the struggle between good and evil to the secondary plane of reality, the world. However, he does not consider evil as "illusory," but takes its threat seriously and emphasizes man's duty to struggle against it.

There are two possible ways of looking at the problem. On the one hand, there is the metaphysical dualism between spirit and matter, between perfection and imperfection, between the Absolute and the relative. On this level evil is understood simply as *"avidyā,"* ignorance which can be overcome through *jnāna,* knowledge. Swami Vivekananda said, "Vedānta recognises no sin, it only recognises error." But in history attention has also to be

---

[15] *Ibid.,* p. 799.

given to the moral dualism between good and evil. The tendency in Radhakrishnan's thought is to consider the struggle between good and evil seriously, but to point out that ultimately the distinction between the two will be transcended. In an important statement on this question he writes:

> These distinctions [of good and evil] belong not to reality as such but to the human world which is part of the cosmic process, which is in itself a phase in which being is alienated from itself. Not that distinctions between good and evil are arbitrary or conventional; they are certainly reasonable and natural, and they express absolute truths of the moral order, but they are fundamentally categories of this world. They are symbolic, not images or shadows.[16]

Thus for Radhakrishnan the struggle between good and evil is to be taken seriously in the practical realm of history; but it is transcended in the ideal realm of true being. In his commentary on the *Gītā* Radhakrishnan further supports this view when he says that "the guided soul leaves behind on earth both good and evil." The immortal man overcomes both the thoughts, "I did evil" and "I did good." "The liberated individual is lifted beyond the ethical distinctions of good and evil."[17] On the basis of statements like these it is difficult to resist the conclusion that in Radhakrishnan's view, the destiny of the individual is to escape from the coils of history and to reach that level when historicity ceases to be and where all distinctions are obliterated.

There is also a tendency in Radhakrishnan as well as in some other modern thinkers to believe that given time and

---

16 *Eastern Religions and Western Thought, op. cit.,* p. 104. See also *An Idealist View of Life, op. cit.,* p. 305.

17 *Bhagavadgītā,* II, 50, quoted in *Religion and Society, op. cit.,* p. 73.

opportunity, evil can be transformed into good. Tagore, for example, compared evil to a child's attempts to walk, implying that it was just a matter of time and growth before the child learned to walk properly. Aurobindo regarded evil as "contrary phenomena," simply a by-product of the evolutionary process. Radhakrishnan also seems to think that the human individual, with proper guidance, discipline, and knowledge can transform evil into good. This is further emphasized by drawing attention to man's freedom.

> To hold that the world consists of free spirits means that evil is possible and probable. . . . If all tendencies to error, ugliness and evil are to be excluded, there can be no seeking of the true, the beautiful and the good. If there is to be an active willing of these ideals of truth, beauty and goodness, then their opposites of error, ugliness and evil are not merely abstract possibilities but positive tendencies which we have to resist.[18]

This, however, seems to make evil necessary in order that man's freedom of choice may have alternatives. But man's freedom itself might be the source of moral evil. Man's abuse of his freedom very often leads to conflicts and tragedies in history. Belief in man's goodness does not always take sufficient account of this possibility. It must also be said that in the course of human history, as freedom is recognized, the possibilities for both good and evil develop with it. If, at the end of history, evil is not destroyed and rejected, but somehow transformed into good, the difference between good and evil would be one of degree and not of kind. Moreover, if there is no possibility of the rejection of evil and the vindication of the good in history, the importance of man's freedom and ethical responsibility would be minimized.

---

[18] *The Bhagavadgītā, op. cit.*, pp. 24–25.

THE MEANING OF "AVATĀRA"

It has already been shown that for Radhakrishnan the world is relatively real, so that the struggle between good and evil is not an illusion. God himself is concerned with this struggle. The significance of the doctrine of *avatāra* must therefore be indicated in this context. When the Eternal appears in time, when God intervenes on the side of *dharma,* it obviously means that God is not indifferent to the struggles in history.

There are two strands in the doctrine of *avatāra* as expounded by Radhakrishnan in his commentary on the *Gītā*. On the one hand, an *avatāra* is a divine intervention in history on the side of the good, to offer deliverance, comfort, and hope to men caught up in the mesh of gigantic evil forces. This is the meaning of the ten classical *avatāras*. On the other hand, according to Radhakrishnan, the *avatāra* is also a demonstration of the divine potentialities of man, showing that through his own self-effort man can achieve divinity here and now. These two emphases are held together in a delicate balance.

The historic context of the *Gītā* is the struggle between *dharma* and *adharma,* the Pandavas representing the former and the Kauravas representing the latter. Krishna, the divine charioteer, is on the side of *dharma.* He is the guide, guardian and friend of *Arjuna,* the hero. Although Krishna himself does not fight, there are enough incidents and indications to prove that he is actively concerned not only with the struggle, but also with its outcome. Radhakrishnan says:

For the *Gītā,* the world is the scene of an active struggle between good and evil in which God is deeply interested. He pours out his wealth of love in helping man to resist all that makes for error, ugliness and evil. As God is completely good and His love boundless, He is concerned about the suffering of the world.[19]

This is in line with the classical view which accepts the plurality of the *avatāras* in accordance with the needs of man at different times in history. "If God is looked upon as the saviour of men, He must manifest Himself, whenever the forces of evil threaten to destroy human values."[20] The *Gītā* itself states this point explicitly in the well-known verses:

Whenever there is a decline of righteousness and rise of unrighteousness, O Bharata, then I send forth myself. For the protection of the good, for the destruction of the wicked and for the establishment of righteousness, I come into being from age to age.[21]

This is the divine *descent* of God into the realm of history.

On the other hand, in the *avatāra* there is also an *ascent* of man into the divine status. Elaborating this point Radhakrishnan says that the *avatāra* "is the demonstration of man's spiritual resources and latent divinity. It is not so much the contraction of divine majesty into the limits of the human frame as the exaltation of human nature to the level of Godhead. . . ." Whenever an individual develops special qualities and starts a spiritual and social revolution in the lives of people around him, one can say that in such a person "God is born." "The incarnation of Krishna is not so much the conversion of Godhead into flesh as the taking up of manhood into God." "The divinity claimed by Krishna is the common reward of all earnest

---

[19] *Ibid.*, p. 25.
[20] *Ibid.*, p. 34.
[21] *Ibid.*, Chapter IV, 7–8.

spiritual seekers. . . . He is not a bygone personality, but the indwelling spirit. . . ."[22] Combining these two aspects, that is, the divine descent and the human ascent to achieve a common purpose in history, Radhakrishnan writes:

> Avatāra means descent, one who has descended. The divine comes down to the earthly plane to raise it to a higher status. God descends when man rises. The purpose of the avatar is to inaugurate a new world, a new dharma. By his teaching and example, he shows how a human being can raise himself to a higher grade of life. The issue between right and wrong is a decisive one. God works on the side of the right. Love and mercy are ultimately more powerful than hatred and cruelty. Dharma will conquer adharma, truth will conquer falsehood; the power behind death, disease and sin will be overthrown by the reality which is Being, Intelligence and Bliss.[23]

It has already been made clear that in Radhakrishnan's view perfection is not attainable in the world of time and space, that true being cannot be revealed in the realm of the secondary plane of reality which is history. Moreover, Radhakrishnan has consistently upheld that it is the personal God alone who incarnates and therefore this sudden reference to "the reality which is Being, Intelligence and Bliss" overthrowing "death, disease and sin" seems inconsistent. It is claimed, however, that Radhakrishnan's view is a spiritual interpretation of history, linking the divine possibilities of man and the actual happenings in history. Analyzing the different views of history, Gokhale points out that in India today there are thinkers like D. P. Mukherji, S. A. Dange, D. D. Kosambi, and others who, following the general theory of Marx, attempt an interpretation of Indian history along Marxist lines. At the other

---

22 *Ibid.*, see pp. 28 ff.
23 *Ibid.*, p. 155.

extreme are men like Radhakrishnan who seek to establish the supremacy of the spirit in history, to whom history is primarily the unfolding of the spirit. In between the two positions stand thinkers like Nehru, who interpret the history of India in personal, romantic, and idealized terms. To the large majority of thinking Indians, however, remarks Gokhale, "History is neither wholly material nor completely spiritual but rather a two dimensional unfolding of the interaction between man and the Supreme Spirit."[24] He makes a significant observation when he says that two views of life—the *ordinary* and the *extraordinary,* interpenetrate the Indian view. History is concerned with the ordinary, the day-to-day happening of human existence; whereas the central affirmation of Indian philosophy is concerned with the extraordinary, the depths of man's selfhood. The doctrine of *avatāra* relates the two. The *nara* of history can become the *narottama* in history and ultimately reach the supreme height of *Nārāyaṇa* who is beyond history.[25] Radhakrishnan's interpretation of the doctrine of *avatāra* lends support to this view, where history assumes cosmic overtones and is regarded essentially as "a narrative exemplifying the fulfilment of eternal values under the active guidance of a Higher Spirit."

"BRAHMA LOKA"—THE END OF HISTORY

The classical Hindu conception of history which is cyclical describes the end as a return to the beginning. The cyclical view with its stress on the inevitable deterioration leading to a *finis,* has no place for the possibility of a *telos*

---

[24] *Indian Thought Through the Ages* (Asia Publishing House, 1961), p. 23.

[25] *Ibid.,* p. 13.

for history. Modern Hindu tendency, if one may generalize, is to recognize the *finis,* but at the same time to describe it in such a way as not to exclude a *telos.* Instead of looking at the movement of history as a process of deterioration, going through the four ages with increasing proportion of *adharma* in each age, finally ending in *praḷaya* (dissolution), history is considered more as a process of spiritual evolution moving toward a culmination. Such an integral or evolutionary view of history attempts to make room for possible fulfillments or ends in history. For Radhakrishnan, the final end is a return to the *Brahman.* Nevertheless, he attempts to show that the life of man and community in the empirical world has value. This is in line with his interpretation of the nature of Ultimate Reality which, though describable in negative terms only, is somehow characterized by value, a point to which attention has already been called. Even as in the West, Socrates and Plato, Bradley and Alexander maintained the ultimate connection between value and reality, so also the idealistic tradition of the Upanishads insists on "the inseparability of value from the truly real."[26] Therefore, the final end and destiny of mankind in history is, in some sense, also a completion and fulfillment.

The destiny of the individual is not just a liberation from the bonds of nature, but a full realization of man's divine potentialities. Such individuals who have attained their destiny are described by Radhakrishnan as *jīvanmuktās,* liberated individuals. After attaining their destiny, according to Radhakrishnan, they do not seek to escape from the world, but take upon themselves "the burden of redeeming the whole world." They transcend their

---

[26] *An Idealist View of Life, op. cit.,* p. 16.

"historic individuality." "Moksha is the realisation of that purpose for each individual. On the attainment of perfection the historical existence terminates. When one individual completes his purpose, he develops the universality of outlook characteristic of perfection, but retains his individuality as a centre of action. When the whole universe reaches its consummation, the liberated individuals lapse into the stillness of the Absolute."[27] Therefore, *moksha* for the individual is "freedom from historicity."

The final end, however, is thought of not in terms of the individual only, but in an emphasis on the community as well. The end is not merely a collection of liberated individuals, but a fellowship, "a new order of beings, and new earth life." It is *brahma loka,* which, being interpreted in Radhakrishnan's words, is the kingdom of God: "Thy kingdom come, is the meaning of history, and the coming of the kingdom is the triumph of meaning."[28] Liberated individuals take upon themselves the burden of redeeming the whole world. When they lead others also into that state, there is *brahma loka,* divine community. It is the life "in which the individuals are united by the perfect interpenetration of mind by mind. . . . Such a state of spiritualised harmony is the end of the world."[29] Though such statements as "lapsing into the stillness of the Absolute," "transcending historic individuality," "spiritualised harmony," and similar ones suggest the identity of the liberated individual with the *Brahman,* Radhakrishnan also says that "equality with God (*sādharmya*) and not identity (*sārupya*), is the characteristic of the end."[30] Moreover, Radhakrishnan conceives of universal salvation, *sarva-*

27 *The Hindu View of Life., op. cit.,* p. 63.
28 "Fragments," p. 45.
29 *The Bhagavadgītā, op. cit.,* p. 76.
30 *Ibid.,* p. 76.

mukti. It is "the perfection of humanity," "the transfiguration of the cosmos." "It is the attainment of wholeness, the overcoming of disruption . . . which we objectify as *Brahma loka*."[31] As to what will happen when finally such a state is reached, Radhakrishnan says, "When the purpose of the cosmos is reached, when the kingdom of God is established . . . then this cosmic process is taken out into that which is beyond all manifestations."[32] Afterward it might be that the Supreme which has in itself infinite possibilities may take other forms of expression in an endless series.

Three observations may be made here. The first is the paradoxical placing together by Radhakrishnan of statements which are difficult to reconcile. Liberated individuality and spiritualized harmony, freedom from historicity and concern for mankind, process and purpose, identity and fellowship, the end of history as a *finis* as also a *telos*—these are exceedingly difficult to hold together within a consistent view of history. To say that this way of looking at some of the major themes of history is "an inter-penetration of the ordinary and the extra-ordinary" leaves the ordinary very precariously on the brink of Being, where it runs the danger of being swallowed up in the infinite depths of the extraordinary. Will such a conception of what Gokhale describes as "a highly intellectualised and spiritualised view of history," with its proportionately greater emphasis on the extraordinary, provide a basis for the ongoing life of India today, where there is a great deal of emphasis on material well-being, social welfare, and political living together? This is a question which not only

31 "Fragments," p. 45.

32 *The Bhagavadgītā*, p. 78.

is not answered by Radhakrishnan, but which deserves serious consideration and study.

The second question is about the historic significance of the individual, a question which obviously ought to be of great importance in a country which stands committed to the democratic way of life. The individual has a twofold relationship. Living in time he has a direct relation to eternity and, at the same time, as part of the community he is also related to its social responsibilities. A one-sided emphasis on the vertical relationship will endanger the social meaning of the individual's life. If *moksha* is understood as "freedom from historicity," to what extent is the individual's destiny responsibly related to the life in society? Moreover, there is always the danger of death cutting off individual life before attaining one's ultimate destiny. The solution of rebirth does not seem to help man as a historic individual, because it offers no continuity of memory, without which the historic character of the individual loses significance.

In the third place, there is the question which can at least be raised theoretically, as to what will happen if the end of history should come before it has reached its fulfillment. In this atomic age, one has to admit the possible danger of an abrupt end to the whole of history. Thus there is the possibility, by no means unreal, of the goal of history being unfulfilled and history coming to an abrupt and capricious end. If this should happen and history as "the vale of values" should cease to exist, what is the basis of hope for mankind?

6. *As Others See Radhakrishnan: an Evaluation*

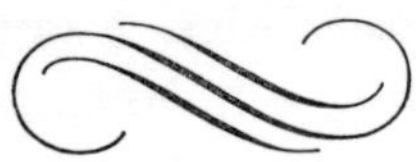

THE ATTEMPT TO EVALUATE THE WORK of any well-known living thinker is beset with many difficulties. For one thing, because the critic does not have a sufficient historic distance between himself and the subject it is not easy to be scrupulously objective. Moreover, when the learned philosopher happens to be not only an eminent thinker, but also the esteemed President of one's own mother country, the task of analyzing his thought and evaluating his work becomes much more difficult. Further, in the case of a living thinker, theoretically at least, there is the possibility of change and growth as a result of which, the conclusions of the critic might run the risk of being based on insufficient data. In the case of Radhakrishnan, however, this is not a serious difficulty because the fundamentals of his system and the general lines of his interpretation have already been worked out in his numerous books. Swami Agehananda Bharati remarks that it is "not only insolent but also unwise to try to pull down what a universally acknowledged specialist has built up in a lifetime."[1]

[1] *The Philosophy of Sarvepalli Radhakrishnan, op. cit.*, p. 478.

Evaluation however, need not necessarily mean pulling down. The responsible critic, while he is being humble in his attitude, cannot at the same time abandon the duty to evaluate the work of a contemporary thinker. In addition to paying a tribute to the greatness of Radhakrishnan in contemporary India, this is a modest attempt, by no means exhaustive, to evaluate some of the basic issues expounded by Radhakrishnan, taking into account the views of some of the representative scholars who have examined the different aspects of his work.

The approach has necessarily to be a selective one to keep oneself within reasonable limits and to avoid the danger of floundering in deeper waters. There is first, the issue of the importance of *fundamentals* and the relevance of *interpretations.* It has been made abundantly clear that Radhakrishnan's major concern is with a restatement of the fundamentals of Hinduism. There are many scholars, particularly contemporary Hindu thinkers, who accept Radhakrishnan's basic approach to Hinduism but would comment on the interpretations given by him of certain classical doctrines. There are others, especially Western Christian theologians, who raise the question of the fundamentals implying thereby that the relevance of the message of Hinduism for today is not just a matter of interpretation, but more seriously one of the adequacy of fundamentals. Here, therefore, the question of religion and religions will be an important question. This leads to a third connected issue, namely, that of *truth* itself in relation to both fundamentals and interpretations. While one is discussing these questions, is one dealing with matters which are simply relative or are there criteria of truth, on the basis of which, one can hold onto absolute validity? One's attitude toward the matter of fusion or fellowship of faiths would very much depend on the answer given to this question, if at all such an answer can logically be given. Apart from these, there are specific issues, like the questions of individuality, personality, community, and the meaning of history, the foundations for which have to be worked out in the life of a nation which has accepted democracy.

THE INDIAN APPRAISAL OF RADHAKHRISHNAN

The appraisal of the work of Radhakrishnan by some of the more important Hindu scholars should be noted. D. S. Sarma in his book[2] devotes a long chapter to Radhakrishnan. To Sarma, Radhakrishnan is "the greatest religious philosopher of modern times" in the true line of descent from the ancient Hindu seers who have, from time to time, rescued the spirit of Hinduism from the onslaughts of secular thought and practice. T. M. P. Mahadevan, in his book dealing with the outlines of Hinduism, makes an appreciative reference to Radhakrishnan in the following words:

> His outspoken championship of the highest values of life in a world which is only too prone to wed the expedient, his clear and firm grasp of the essentials of religion, and the untiring zeal with which he has been exhorting men of faith to emphasise these essentials rather than the accidents of belief, his insistence on the correct understanding of Hinduism and of its attitude of genuine hospitality towards other religions—these have marked him out as a great force making a significant contribution to the emergence of a new India and a new world.[3]

---

[2] D. S. Sarma, *The Renaissance of Hinduism* (Banaras: Hindu University Press, 1944), pp. 585 ff.

[3] T. M. P. Mahadevan, *Outlines of Hinduism* (Bombay: Chetana, Ltd., 1956), p. 286.

This is high praise indeed and certainly justified when one takes into account the needs of modern India and the life-work of Radhakrishnan. Both Sarma and Mahadevan consider him not only as an interpreter of Hinduism alone, but at the same time, as "the defender of the religious faith of mankind," because they accept Radhakrishnan's thesis that "all religions are one in essence." In other words, as far as the fundamentals of Hinduism are concerned, they are in agreement with Radhakrishnan. Their opinion, however, is not a critical examination of Radhakrishnan's thought, but primarily an exposition based on approval and acceptance. In a recent book already mentioned, B. G. Gokhale also refers to Radhakrishnan in several contexts. In dealing with the Indian view of history, Gokhale groups Radhakrishnan with Aurobindo and Gandhi, arguing that they take up "where ancient India left off and work out the spiritual view of history as developed by ancient Indian thinkers . . . into a consistent, logical, and imperative philosophy of history."[4] This means that Gokhale also accepts the line of continuity in Hindu fundamentals and basic approach from the *Vedas* to Radhakrishnan.

There are other scholars, however, who are critical of Radhakrishnan's thought. Scholars like Nagaraja Sarma and P. N. Srinivasa Sastri have been critical of his system on different grounds. In the authoritative volume on Radhakrishnan edited by Schilpp, to which reference has already been made, Swami Agehananda Bharati, the Austrian scholar who has become a Hindu monk, discusses the characteristics of theology and philosophy and concludes that "Radhakrishnan is a theologian and that *he is*

---

[4] *Op. cit.*, p. 21.

the theologian of Hinduism."[5] The Swami claims that this is "the highest tribute a monk can pay a layman," although his implied criticism seems to be that what Radhakrishnan is building is not philosophy. Without getting involved in the intricate question of the relation between philosophy and theology or in the other question of the characteristics of a philosophy of religion, it may be observed here that to the learned Swami, Radhakrishnan is a theologian because, in the Swami's opinion, *Vedānta* itself is theology on the ground that it puts its entire emphasis on ontology and metaphysics. His assessment of Radhakrishnan's work is based on this conviction, which, however, may not be acceptable to others. P. T. Raju and D. M. Datta are more critical both of the substance and the method of Radhakrishnan. To Raju, Radhakrishnan is the protagonist of a new school of cultural synthesis, of a new humanism,[6] in which not all the elements seem to be derived from the classical Hindu tradition. According to him, Radhakrishnan's major contribution lies in the realm of Indian epistemology, of comparative philosophy, and in the shaping of a world philosophy. Datta, discussing primarily Radhakrishnan's interpretation of Indian philosophy, draws attention gently but firmly to "the intolerable ambiguity" in certain areas of Radhakrishnan's work because of a lack of precision in the use of certain words and an absence of definition of certain key terms. This, however, is not all the fault of Radhakrishnan, because some of these time-honored words and terms in general vogue are used by different people in a variety of ways. In answer to the question whether Radhakrishnan is

[5] *The Philosophy of Sarvepalli Radhakrishnan, op. cit.,* p. 465.
[6] *Ibid.,* pp. 515 ff.

a faithful interpreter of Indian philosophy, Datta rightly observes that the same question might be asked of many other writers also, as, for example, Dasgupta, Hiriyanna, and others; and he points out that "no exposition of good sense can help interpreting what *he thinks* would be fair to the original writer."[7]

M. N. Roy, being an avowed Marxist, certainly cannot be regarded as a believing Hindu and his philosophic position naturally influences his appraisal of Radhakrishnan.[8] Discussing Radhakrishnan in the perspective of Indian philosophy, Roy remarks that "there is nothing peculiarly Hindu" in his thought and seriously questions the description of the Hindu view of life as "spiritual." He maintains that in the long process of the development of Indian philosophy, the naturalist, rationalist, skeptic, agnostic, and materialist trends of thought should not be ignored. According to him India remained "spiritual" because of historical reasons, particularly because she was deprived of the benefits of modern science. This is not the place to examine Roy's contention, nor is it necessary to do so for the purpose of this work. There is, however, considerable truth in his point of view; although it must also be said that Radhakrishnan himself has not denied the existence and importance of these trends in the structure of Indian philosophic thought. The conclusion of this brief review is that although there are a few Hindu scholars who are highly critical of his position, the majority of the Hindu scholars are less critical and more appreciative of both the substance of Radhakrishnan's thought and the method of his interpretation.

---

7 *Ibid.*, p. 675.
8 *Ibid.*, pp. 543 ff.

THE CHRISTIAN THEOLOGIANS AND THE HINDU PHILOSOPHER

Fundamentals and interpretations are closely connected. To what extent Radhakrishnan is faithful to the basic doctrines of Hinduism, is a question which is often raised. Radhakrishnan's interpretation of the time-honored Hindu concepts like the *Brahman, karma, māyā* and others gives the impression that although the forms are the same, the content put into these words is full of new religious meaning, so that Devanandan is justified in observing that the Hinduism of Radhakrishnan is "Hinduism reborn—a new creation, not merely revived and reconstructed. . . . It is prophetic of a religious theory yet unborn to justify the practice of today."[9] He raises the question whether it will be possible for Hinduism to produce from the depths of its own religious resources "an articulate, reasoned system, an adequate creed as a basis of belief, which will provide the needed intellectual justification and spiritual drive for this new Hindu way of life."[10] The same question is also put by Stephen Neill when, discussing the new patterns of renascent Hinduism, he asks:

> But is this what Hinduism really is? Are the springs of men's action today really the inherited beliefs to which with greater or less conviction they profess adherence . . . ? Has Hinduism within itself the vitality to produce both the intellectual categories in which the new understanding of life can be expressed, and the spiritual power through which the exciting vision can be realised?[11]

---

[9] *The Concept of Māyā* (London: Lutterworth Press, 1950), p. 227–228.

[10] *Ibid.*, p. 230. See also the same author's *Resurgent Hinduism* (Bangalore, India: Christian Institute for the Study of Religion and Society, 1958), pp. 18 ff.

[11] Stephen Neill, *Christian Faith and Other Faiths* (London: Oxford University Press, 1962), p. 81. Used by permission.

This question, therefore, deals not just with the relevance of modern interpretations, but with the *adequacy* of ancient fundamentals. Can such a question be asked? What is the basis on which it can legitimately be raised? What are the criteria with reference to which adequacy or inadequacy is determined? The question of fundamentals can be raised only at the level of faith and commitment. In this connection, the opinions of three outstanding Christian theologians—Newbigin, Kraemer, and Neill—who have criticized some of the basic affirmations of Radhakrishnan's thought, and therefore of Hinduism itself, might be considered here. Both Newbigin and Neill are well-known theologians who were in India for many years and have firsthand contact with modern Hindu thought and practice. Kraemer is an acknowledged authority on Eastern religions, whose profound scholarship and mature insights command the respect of even those who may not fully agree with his judgments.

Newbigin's consideration of Radhakrishnan is on the question of the basis for a world faith,[12] and touches one of the most important issues in the encounter between world religions today. He takes strong exception to the claims of Hinduism put forward by Radhakrishnan. The claim that the inner essence of all religions is the same, though it is an almost official dogma and national policy in India today, is not a modern doctrine. It was already stated in the *Gītā* where Krishna declares that he is in every religion as the thread through a string of pearls. Much earlier than that, the *Rig Veda* states that Reality is One, though the sages call it many. In modern times Ramakrishna gently affirms it. Vivekananda proclaimed it all

---

12 *A Faith for This One World?* (London: Student Christian Movement Press, Limited, 1961).

over the world in ringing tones. In contemporary India Radhakrishnan is the ablest and most persuasive exponent of this doctrine, according to which it is the *Vedānta* that can provide the ultimate basis for a world faith. Pointing out that a religion which claims to offer a foundation for a world faith should necessarily have a basis for community, Newbigin remarks that the emphasis on mystical experience so strongly advocated by Radhakrishnan is too individualistic to provide that basis. The Unity it offers is "the negative unity of tolerance rather than the positive unity of love." Emphasizing this familiar point Newbigin remarks:

> But so long as the central and controlling idea is salvation through the knowledge of identity with the Supreme Self, so long as the world of multiplicity and change is believed to be unreal, Hinduism can never put a visible human community into the centre of its creed, as Christianity puts the Church. The unity which it offers is the cessation of strife, not the creation of a new community.[13]

Moreover, according to Newbigin, Radhakrishnan's claim that truth transcends historic particularities is "a declaration of war upon all religion which claims to be based upon a historic revelation." This, it is pointed out, is the dividing line between religions, not a bridge of unity. He goes on to remark,

> The claim that the Vedānta is the truth transcending all religions is necessarily a flat denial of the central truth of biblical religion. The reality of the mystical experience need not be denied, and indeed, cannot be; but the assertion that it is the clue to reality is an affirmation of faith which must be

[13] *Ibid.*, pp. 40–41.

judged by the criteria that are proper in the field of religious belief.[14]

With reference to some of Newbigin's remarks one may raise the question whether it is justifiable to consider Radhakrishnan as the exponent of a "world faith." What Radhakrishnan seems to advocate strongly is, in his own words, "a fellowship not a fusion of faiths." The structure and basis for a fellowship of faiths need not be the same as that for a world faith. Further, Radhakrishnan does not seem to question the *validity* of the Christian faith. What he objects to is what appears to him to be the *exclusiveness* of the Christian claim. Without surrendering one's cherished convictions, it is necessary to recognize this distinction. A call for co-operation among religions and for a fellowship of faiths can hardly be described as "a declaration of war upon all religion based upon a historic revelation." At no time in the encounter among world religions is a sympathetic understanding of other faiths more necessary than today when religious values are under the incessant attacks of the powerful forces of materialism.

H. Kraemer considers Radhakrishnan so important that he gives a full section to an analysis and criticism of his thought. He believes Radhakrishnan to be representative of the Indian way of thinking.[15] It is unfortunate, however, that Kraemer's expressions are too strong, particularly when he speaks of what he considers to be the basic weakness and insincerity of Hinduism. A scholar of the caliber of Kraemer is entitled to his opinions, but one frankly wishes that he could have avoided terms like "insincerity" in this connection; because, in spite of his careful ex-

---

14 *Ibid.*, pp. 39–40.

15 Hendrik Kraemer, *Religion and the Christian Faith* (London: Lutterworth Press, 1956; and Philadelphia: The Westminster Press, 1957).

planation of what he means, it is obviously liable to be misunderstood by both Hindu and non-Hindu readers. Kraemer argues that the weakness of Hindu fundamentals lies in two facts: first, because it makes man's experience the main ground for the finality of truth; and, second, because it reduces all forms of religion and morality to the status of being mere instruments to an end. Religiously speaking it amounts to "obliterating God and putting man in his place. *Ātman* swallows the *Brahman*. . . . So religion, in principle, becomes a means for psychological satisfaction and utility. Here lies . . . the blind spot of Hindu spirituality." Further, he says, "In India, it seems, the emphasis on the quest of truth has been imperceptibly shifted from truth to liberation, from *satya* the objective, to *mukti* the subjective."[16] He claims that Ramanuja's criticism of Sankara was the protest of a sincere religious soul against "the ultimately religious insincerity of Sankara's system." Analyzing Radhakrishnan's mind, Kraemer says that so far as Christianity is concerned he has misunderstood it completely. He looks *at* Christianity, not *into* Christianity. Radhakrishnan's real concern is with not "the problem of truth but the cultural and social eminence of Hinduism." In Hinduism as interpreted by Radhakrishnan there is a mystic individualism which permits no responsible emphasis on community problems. Moreover, Radhakrishnan's call for co-operation among religions amounts to "a gentle herding of tame sheep into a common pen." Firmly rejecting this call, Kraemer observes,

What is needed in the present time of world-encounter of religions is not to be as sweet as possible with each other, but to

---

[16] *Ibid.*, pp. 111–113.

learn the art of being as true as possible with each other in spiritual emulation.[17]

Stephen Neill, in a chapter characterized by informed understanding and balanced judgment, takes into account the historical background of Radhakrishnan. Hinduism has reacted in different ways to the acids of modernity. People recognized the values in Western culture, but were also responsibly critical both of its content and forms of expression. There was the reaction of refusal, more emotional than intellectual, vigorously represented by Dayananda Saraswati, who sought to preserve the old at all costs. There were also others whose reaction may rightly be described as warm welcome, who tried to make a deliberate attempt to work out a syncretistic faith. Raja Ram Mohan Roy was highly appreciative and strongly critical of Western values. The third reaction, more difficult to define, but nonetheless perhaps more significant, is the deliberate attempt to reinterpret Hinduism and justify its ancient values in the context of modern needs. Neill thinks that Radhakrishnan is the best example of this reaction and the most important creator of modern Hinduism. He agrees with Kraemer, however, that Radhakrishnan misunderstands Christianity and that his attitude is one of more than thorough dislike. Moreover, in Radhakrishnan, Hinduism has evidently become conscious of its superiority. To him "the Eastern wisdom as communicated in the Hindu Vedānta is not merely superior to any other, but will be found to be of universal significance."[18] Radhakrishnan's call for tolerance and co-operation among religions is based on the assumption that truth is essentially

---

17 *Ibid.*, p. 134. Used by permission of The Westminster Press, Philadelphia.

18 *Christian Faith and Other Faiths*, *op. cit.*, p. 83.

unknowable and that all religions can only be approximations to the truth, and so are relative. The root principle in the matter of possible relation among religions ought therefore to be *sarvāgamaprāmaṇya,* the truth and authority of all religions. Recognizing the influence which Radhakrishnan undoubtedly continues to exercise in contemporary India, Neill writes:

> The sense of mystery which to so large an extent has been lost in pragmatic Western religion, the call to freedom of a quest in place of the inhibiting reliance of dogma, the broad genial tolerance which is prepared to find a place for everything, the respect for the individual which encourages him to find his own spiritual way . . . by such expositions of the Hindu faith as this it has been possible to restore Hindu self-respect . . . But this does not answer some of the burning questions that must arise with the changed attitude and situation of India today.[19]

One hopes that this brief summary is a fair presentation of the points of view of these outstanding theologians and an indication of the main points of their disagreement with Radhakrishnan. Certain observations could be made here, drawing attention to some of the issues involved in this encounter.

SOME IMPORTANT ISSUES

The first observation is on the question of the *adequacy* of Hindu fundamentals to meet the demands of the modern age. The question is asked, Has Hinduism within itself the vitality to produce the spiritual power and intellectual categories to realize the glorious vision which is being defined for the India of today? The form in which this

---

[19] *Christian Faith and Other Faiths* (London: Oxford University Press, 1962), pp. 85–86. Used by permission.

question is sometimes articulated is understandably irritating to the Hindu. If a Christian in the West were to be repeatedly questioned about the adequacy of Christian fundamentals to meet modern needs, he would probably react in the same manner. Now, *adequacy* is something which can be determined only with reference to specific human needs. In the realm of religion it must take into account man's spiritual needs and his commitment to a faith or no faith. If the modern Hindu is not particularly concerned with the gap between his ancient faith and modern practice or, if he claims, as many do, that the present restatement of his ancestral beliefs is, as far as he is concerned, fully adequate to justify his practices, how can someone standing outside the circle of his faith question the adequacy or inadequacy of *his* faith? Devanandan, in an earlier work discussing the "dynamic rejuvenation of Hinduism" as represented by Radhakrishnan observed that in these modern Hindu interpretations "the original postulates of Hindu Upanishadic orthodoxy are indeed retained, but to serve an altogether different purpose, as containers, rather than as generators." In other words, he recognized the usefulness of old bottles, but questioned the adequacy of the old wine. Writing nearly eight years later and again discussing Radhakrishnan, he seems to be less critical of him on this score. Admitting that Radhakrishnan is the most brilliant exponent of Neo-Vedānta, Devanandan writes, "Reform is based on and related to the past. So he would build on the foundations of Vedānta."[20] Does this mean that the question of the adequacy of the Hindu ancestral faith is less important now and that what is really important to the Hindu today is his present practice?

---

[20] See P. D. Devanandan, *The Concept of Māyā, op. cit.,* 1950, p. 231 and *Resurgent Hinduism, op. cit.,* 1958, p. 20.

Surely, one has to recognize the connection between the present way of life and the ancient view of life, but that does not necessarily mean questioning the adequacy of restated fundamentals.

A second issue is the glaring gap between mystical experience and historic faith. At present, the gap between Hindu philosophers and most of the Christian theologians is so wide that any hope of building a bridge seems to be doomed to failure from the very beginning. If mystical experience is the stumbling block to the Christian theologian, historicity is the stumbling block to the Hindu philosopher. Though the reality of mystical experience is not questioned, the assertion that it can be a clue to reality is rejected by the theologians. On the other hand, although history might manifest relative forms of truth, a historical fact can never become to the Hindu philosophers the vehicle of final revelation. There is, of course, considerable misunderstanding of terms like historicity, finality, experience, and revelation. Nevertheless, the difference is fundamental. Tillich has pointed out that mystic religion need not contradict, but possibly does intensify prophetic religion. How this can be done is a different question. But there is one issue here which is of greater significance: namely, the search for a basis for world community or even a fellowship of faiths. The claim that mystical experience, because it is universal, can provide this basis is difficult to accept because mystical experience, by its very nature, is individualistic. It may generate tolerance and courtesy toward similar experiences of others; but can it lead to corporate expression? In contrast, a historic fact, because it has become meaningful to a group, a community, or a nation, inevitably leads to corporate loyalty and efforts. Mahatma Gandhi's experience does not serve as a basis for common loyalty. But the historic fact of his life and his work has drawn together people of different communities and has served to give the nation a common loyalty. Without minimizing the reality and importance of mystical experience, one has to express doubts about its possibility to provide the basis and inspiration to an ongoing community life.

A third observation is with regard to the interpretation of some of the classical doctrines of Hinduism by Radhakrishnan. Modern Vedāntins are keenly aware of the fact that if *māyā* means that the world is illusory, if *karma* is only deterministic and if caste is a rigid structure based on birth only, human life would have little meaning. Now, Radhakrishnan himself has said repeatedly that he has interpreted *māyā* so as "to save the reality of the world," that *karma* is a condition, not a destiny, and that in a growing society, what is significant is not the structure, but the principle of caste. Should not his intention and effort be given more adequate recognition and greater appreciation? Granting that Sankara's doctrine of *māyā* did lend itself to an illusory theory of the world—the very vehemence with which Radhakrishnan defends Sankara is an indication of it—is it justifiable to repeat the charge that to Radhakrishnan "the tangible world is *māyā,* illusory" when he himself says that all that he means by the term is simply that the world is "relatively real"? Also, one should not ignore the fact that in the exposition of the Hindu doctrine of God as expounded by Radhakrishnan there is considerable emphasis on the value content of the *Brahman.* This is true even in the *Upanishads* in spite of the negative descriptions. Therefore the question why, to the Vedāntin "It," *Tat* is more true than "He," why the impersonal is a more inclusive category than the personal, should perhaps be formulated differently, taking Radhakrishnan's conception of *Īśvara* into more serious account.

There is a recognition in Radhakrishnan as well as in other modern Hindu thinkers that an understanding of the world as a realm of meaningful purpose and a doctrine of man as a free and worthy individual, cannot be shaped without a corresponding working out of a doctrine of God as Creator, Lord, and Savior. This is the reason why for Radhakrishnan, though *philosophically Brahman* is the ultimate concept, *pragmatically Īśvara* is Creator, Lord and Savior. This, however, does not necessarily mean that a modern Hindu doctrine of God, of man and the world have all been worked out; it simply means that a greater appreciation of what is being done and a more sympathetic recognition of future possibilities should not be lost sight of. Kraemer is quite right when he says that in the present encounter among religions what is necessary is "not to be as sweet as possible" with each other, but "to be as true as possible" in one's ultimate devotion to God as Truth. This obviously applies both ways and leads to the important question of the relation between religion, religions, and truth.

RELIGION, RELIGIONS, AND TRUTH

The relation on the one hand between religion and Truth and on the other between the different religions, is one of the most complicated issues that are being discussed today. The striking absence of unanimity on this question among scholars of acknowledged learning and unquestioned integrity is an indication both of the importance and the complexity of the subject. The differences in points of view, the absences of precise definitions, and the lack of universally accepted criteria of judgment make a consideration of this subject more difficult. It does not take long to discover that there are differences in the matter defining truth and the essence of religion. Whether it is possible at all to extract and define the essence of religion apart from its historic expression, and whether truth in the ultimate sense is definable, is also a question on which there is no agreement. Moreover, since the issues involved deal with fundamental principles, people rightly hesitate to ignore cherished convictions for the sake of a dubious friendliness.

A brief reference is here made to the idea of a fellowship of faiths so strongly advocated by Radhakrishnan. The call for interreligious co-operation cannot ignore the question of truth, but simply makes it more urgent and important. The idea of a Parliament of Religions is not new. Ever since Swami Vivekananda represented Hinduism at Chicago in 1893, this idea has commanded a great deal of emotional enthusiasm and intellectual interest in India. Radhakrishnan has consistently pleaded not only for a meeting of the religions, but a fellowship of faiths. His convictions on this matter have not changed, and his interest has not waned during the years. The international Union for the Study of Great Religions (USGR) is an extension of this idea having for its objective "a revised religious ideal for man as a social being in this life." The India section of the USGR held a seminar at Bangalore in 1955 on "The Great Scriptures" and another at Madras in 1956 on "The Saints." Radhakrishnan is the President for the Area Committee for India of the USGR and continues to give his unstinted support to the work of the movement. This indicates that the need for a more informed understanding of the subject is being increasingly recognized. It also means that the possibility of interreligious co-operation on a deeper level can be raised only when there is greater recognition of the relation between religion and truth.

One of the most searching examinations of this question has been done by D. G. Moses[21] who devotes an important chapter to Radhakrishnan, analyzing his thought and bringing out some of the basic issues involved, issues which are sometimes ignored in the haze of friendliness or obscured in the heat of controversy. Two questions may be raised in this connection. What are the special characteristics of religious truth; and, second, what is the relation between religious truth and the religions? There is certainly a distinct relationship between religious truth and religious experience, but it cannot be said that religious truth is the result of religious experience. Religious experience already implies the existence of religious truth. One has, however, to recognize that religious experience is related to religious truth. One of the major differences between scientific truth and religious truth is in the matter of communicability. In science, communication is possible through precise definitions and exact terms which are capable of verification and demonstration. On the basis of such universally accepted means of communication and norms of judgment it is easy to establish a universal community. In the case of scientific truth "subjective certitude coincides with objective certainty." But a religious individual may have subjective certitude; nevertheless, his belief may lack objective validity. Yet, merely because of this, one cannot dismiss religious beliefs as false. The difficulty in communication, therefore, is the dilemma of all religious knowledge. There are several reasons why religious truths cannot be obtrusively objective.

---

21 *Religious Truth and the Relation Between Religions,* United Society for Christian Literature, Madras, 1950.

First, religious truths are not immediately relevant to man's physical existence. Man may not recognize that they are necessary to his day-to-day life. It is quite possible to live without a conscious recognition of the realities of religion. Second, religious truths, to be accepted, need a prior preparation. Unless one has a spiritual sensitivity, particularly a sense of the moral quality of loyalty to truth at all costs, a person might remain quite unaware of and insensitive to truth. Lastly, religious truths cannot be forced upon others. Like all other spiritual gifts they have to be voluntarily accepted. These differences between religious and scientific truth are important and should not be lost sight of.

Radhakrishnan's conception of religious truth and the relation among religions is carefully stated in the chapter entitled "The Meeting of Religions" in the book *Eastern Religions and Western Thought*. This, however, was written in 1939, and in his later works Radhakrishnan discusses this theme taking into account some of the more recent criticisms, notably in his "Reply" to Critics (1952) and in his *Recovery of Faith* (1955). Radhakrishnan's main argument may be briefly summarized thus. *Sat* or *Truth* is One, fathomless and all-inclusive. All religions are merely approximations to truth. No single religion can claim finality in its possession of truth. Consequently, the claim to uniqueness or exclusiveness by any particular religion should be given up. The relation among religions should be one of understanding and co-operation rather than one of competition and strife.

There are several affirmations involved in Radhakrishnan's position. The first point is that truth is one and all-inclusive and that all religions are approximations to it. "The different creeds are historical formulation of formless truth." "The absoluteness of truth implies the relativity of all forms of truth." There is a common element which is the foundation for all religions, but the building erected on this foundation differs. "God's architecture is not of a standard pattern."[22] With reference to this, two questions may be raised. First, the meaning of the term "all-inclusiveness" and also why it should be considered the supreme characteristic of reality. If *Sat* were mere Being, then it would be boundless and characterless. Can *Sat* be so all-inclusive that it includes within itself even the demonic forces considered gods by certain religions? Moreover, to speak about the absoluteness and relativity of truth, Truth as it is and approximations to truth, seems to be self-contradictory because it implies that man has two kinds of knowledge—that of reality as it is and that of the approximations also. How can one talk about approximations unless one also knows the Absolute, with reference to which, they can be called approximations? This is a valid observation dealing with the possibility of religious knowledge.

Second, there is the affirmation that since Reality is fullness of truth or fathomless or absolute, historic religions have to be content with symbols and no one symbol can claim superiority over another. It implies that Reality cannot be known in conceptual terms. Radhakrishnan calls mankind "to rise to the conception of a God above gods, who is beyond image and concept, who can be experienced, but not known." It is true that one should acknowledge that God is beyond image and concept, that Truth is greater than man's reach and that the human mind cannot comprehend the fullness of God. But whereas such an attitude should make man humble before the ultimate mystery of God, it should not preclude the funda-

[22] *The Recovery of Faith, op. cit.*, p. 188. See also "Reply," pp. 804 ff.

mental assumption that Reality is knowable, without which all knowledge will be strangled at birth. The relationship among religions on the basis of a unity of quest leading to the familiar statement that all religions are equally useful pathways to God is liable to mislead. All paths do not necessarily lead to the mountain top. Some might be blind alleys, some might lead away from the top. To give to all the same status would be unreasonable. Therefore, even if one might concede that no religion is devoid of some truth, it does not mean that all religions have the same degree of truth.

The third assertion concerns the question of finality. Radhakrishnan vigorously argues that no particular religion can claim finality. According to him the claim to the possession of a unique, revealed truth which declines to be classified as one among the many leads to aggression and is ruinous for co-operation among religions. It must be recognized that any attitude of aggressive superiority would go against the spirit of religion itself. However, the claim of finality would depend on what one means by "finality." If by finality is meant a complete comprehension of God, the last word in religion, then obviously no particular historical religion can claim such a thing. On the other hand, if by final, one means *fundamental,* that which is elemental or that which is absolutely essential, then it should be possible for even a historic religion to claim finality. It is like the finality of a basic chord of music without which no harmony can ever be worked out and which serves as the basis for further musical compositions. This way of looking at finality is not incompatible with the finitude of man nor does it exclude further progress. Neither need it lead to the exclusiveness of arrogant possession.

An observation regarding the conception of truth may be made here. It looks as if to the Hindu thinkers, including Radhakrishnan, Truth is more a state of being than an experience of cognition. *Brahman* is *Sat,* Being and at the same time also *Satyam,* truth. This identification of being and truth leads to a difference both in one's mode of thinking and one's conception of *mukti. Mukti* is not just freedom from untruth, it is true being. When it is recognized that Truth is One, are these two points of view irreconcilable? Are there two modes of knowing, one in the East and one in the West? Is one preoccupied with the less determinate facts of existence and the other with the more determinate facts of essence? Radhakrishnan himself recognizes this possibility, but believes that it should not be difficult to establish a world community in which the two sets of values derived from the two modes of knowing are to be reconciled.

CONCLUSION

It is of great significance to the future that India has chosen the way of democracy and is now in the process of working out a basis which should provide stability to its foundations, inspiration for its efforts, and a sense of direction to its national goals. Whether the lasting contribution to the shaping of that basis will be provided by the secular philosophies or by the religio-philosophic traditions of India is a question which will assume increasing importance in the years that are ahead. The importance of Radhakrishnan is to be found in his untiring work to draw the attention of the nation to its spiritual resources.

What has been attempted here is not merely an exposition but, as far as possible, a critical interpretation of the essentials of Radhakrishnan's thought. Radhakrishnan has recently been elected to the highest office which a nation can bestow on its citizen—that of the President of the Indian Republic. The satisfaction and hope with which this election was received both in India and abroad is an indication of the importance of Radhakrishnan not only as a philosopher, but also as a statesman. The years ahead will surely give him more opportunity to influence the thinking of the Government at the highest level and to shape the mind of the nation. Therefore, an attempt to understand the essentials of his thought is, to a considerable extent, an attempt to understand the life and thought of modern India itself. In this sense he is the representative of the renaissance in India today. At the same time to seek to understand his religious and philosophic thought, is also to enter into the complex structure of contemporary Hinduism. The march of events, both in the world and in the national life of the country, has undoubtedly affected the very core of Hinduism, which is seeking to adjust itself to the national awakening in all areas of life. Radhakrishnan is not merely a product of this national awakening, but has also in a real measure contributed to its movement, character, and direction. It needs informed understanding, sympathetic appreciation, balanced judgment, and a willingness to step out of one's accustomed modes of thinking to appreciate what is so significantly happening both in the life of the nation and in the living structure of Hinduism. We need to move from the position of mere confrontation to that of real communication, so that a responsible dialogue among peoples of different countries and different persuasions would be not only possible, but also meaningful in the world today.

Selected Bibliography

This bibliography is not exhaustive, but represents a selection from the more important books of Sarvepalli Radhakrishnan.

1. *The Reign of Religion in Contemporary Philosophy* (London: Macmillan & Co., Ltd. 1920). This starts with a discussion on the relation between science, religion, and philosophy, examines the views of thinkers like Bergson, James, and Bertrand Russell, and offers Radhakrishnan's suggestions for an approach to Reality based on the Upanishads.

2. *Indian Philosophy* (London: Allen & Unwin, Ltd.), Volume I, 1st Edition, 1923. Revised Edition, 1929. Volume II, 1st Edition, 1927. Revised Edition, 1931. Also (New York: The Macmillan Company, 2 vols., 1923–1927). A comprehensive treatment of the historical development and the essential characteristics of Indian philosophy.

3. *The Hindu View of Life* (London: Allen & Unwin, Ltd., 1927; and New York: The Macmillan Company). Upton lectures delivered at Oxford. Several reprints, the most recent one being a paperback edition by the same publishers. This is perhaps the best introduction to Radhakrishnan's thought and to contemporary Hinduism. Deals with the nature and content of religious experience, discusses the Hindu attitude toward the relation between religions, and has two important chapters on Hindu *dharma,* interpreting the Hindu ideal of man and society.

4. *An Idealist View of Life,* Hibbert Lectures for 1929 (London: Allen & Unwin, Ltd.; and New York: The Macmillan Company). Third impression, 1947. Discusses the relevance of religion in an age of science, dealing with the affirmations of religious experience and the nature and destiny of human personality.

5. *East and West in Religion* (London: Allen & Unwin, Ltd.; and New York: The Macmillan Company). First published, 1933. Second impression, 1949. A comparative study, examining some of the major issues involved.

6. *Eastern Religions and Western Thought,* Humphrey and Milford, eds. (Oxford, Eng.: The Clarendon Press, 1939; New York: Oxford University Press, 1940). This book is one of the most important works of Radhakrishnan, giving a clue to his attitude to fundamental issues. Discusses the supreme spiritual ideal of the

Hindus, defends the Hindu view of the world against Western criticisms, attempts to establish the validity of mysticism, describes and interprets the individual and social order in Hinduism, and strongly pleads for a meeting of religions on the basis of tolerance and mutual understanding.

7. *Religion and Society* (London: Allen & Unwin, Ltd., 1942; and New York: The Macmillan Company). Second Edition, 1948. Kamala lectures delivered at Calcutta. Deals with the interrelation between the foundations of religion and the structure of society, discussing such topics as the need for religion, women in Hindu society, and war and nonviolence.

8. *The Bhagavadgītā* (London: Allen & Unwin, Ltd., Second Edition, 1949; and Harper & Row, New York). Introductory Essay, Sanskrit text, English translation, and notes. The introductory essay is most helpful in understanding Radhakrishnan's thought on the nature and destiny of man, the status of the world, and the doctrine of *avatāra.*

9. "Fragments of a Confession: The Religion of the Spirit and the World's Need" and "Reply to Critics" are two important essays in *The Philosophy of Radhakrishnan,* Paul A. Schilpp, ed. (New York: Tudor Publishing House, 1952; after January 1, 1964, LaSalle, Ill.: Open Court Publishing Company). These essays contain some of the mature reflections of Radhakrishnan, the first dealing with some of the formative factors and the second discussing the major issues with his critics.

10. *The Principal Upanishads* (London: Allen & Unwin, Ltd., 1953). Edited by Radhakrishnan with introduction, text, translation, and notes. Deals with the important teachings of the Upanishads.

11. *The Recovery of Faith.* World Perspective Series (New York: Harper & Row, Inc. 1955). Attempts a justification of religion and defines the characteristics of the religion that ought to be relevant in an age of atomic science. Analyzes the difficulties of belief, emphasizes the need for belief, discusses the relation between religious truth and symbolism, and pleads for an interreligious friendship on a world level.

12. *The Brahma Sūtra,* The Philosophy of Spiritual Life (London: Allen & Unwin, Ltd., 1960). The latest important book by Radhakrishnan. Introduction, text translation, and notes. Attempts to relate the basic teachings of a great Hindu classic to the situations created by the historical forces of the present. Claims to be a contribution to the development of solidarity of thought in the modern world.

ABOUT THE AUTHOR

Born in 1920, Dr. S. J. Samartha had his college education in the University of Madras, from where he took a degree in Economics and History. After completing his basic theological training at the United Theological College, Bangalore, he worked for some years as a lecturer in systematic theology and history of religions. Selected to go abroad for further studies, he did postgraduate work at the Union Theological Seminary, New York, the Hartford Seminary Foundation, Hartford, Conn., and at the University of Basel, Switzerland. He earned the degree of Doctor of Philosophy in 1958 with a dissertation entitled "The Modern Hindu View of History," part of which has been published under the title, *The Hindu View of History: Classical and Modern*. His articles have been published in reputed journals in India and abroad. At present Dr. Samartha is the Professor of Philosophy and History of Religions as well as the Director, Department of Research and Postgraduate Studies at the United Theological College, Bangalore, South India. He also serves as the General Editor of the Christian Students' Library, which is a basic textbook series published for the Senate of Serampore University, India.

Von Canon Library
146605
REMOTE B 133 .R16 S3 / Introduction to Radhakrishnan